Wide Awake

The Untold Stories of Greatness

P. Shandip Sabapathy

notionpress.com

INDIA • SINGAPORE • MALAYSIA

ISBN 979-8-89724-877-3

– To my parents.

FIRST THINGS FIRST

I don't have a clichéd quote on gratitude to share here, but I have many people to thank and an abundance of gratitude to express!

Mrs. P. Krishnaveni:

She is my first love, my best friend, my finest teacher, and my favourite storyteller. She has stayed wide awake all these years, protecting and nurturing me. Thank you, Amma, for making me who I am today!

Mr. Paramasivam C. N:

He is my first hero, my wisest mentor, my strongest ally, and my greatest cheerleader. It is his dream that I write such a book. Thank you, Appa, for all the values, wisdom, and goodness you've sown in me!

Once the first draft was ready, you took ownership of the book and went all out to see it reach the finish line. Just as Hermione from the Harry Potter series seamlessly juggles a dozen classes, you managed every process—from correspondence to proofreading. Thank you, Srinidhi Vinod, for being that sweet sister who goes all out to support her brother!

Mr. Vinod R. Malya:

Out of the blue, I asked you for a cover page, and you poured your heart into the book cover! And even without my asking, you enhanced the quality of my writing with your exceptional prowess. I've always believed that the beauty of your heart translates into the beauty of your art. Thank you, Anna, for being the finest piece of art I've ever come across!

A tree is only as strong as its roots. Thank you to Harish Raghuraman, R. K. Karthikeyan, Prem Rajan, Priyanka Aswin, Manickam Maalan Barathi, Lakshmanan Arasu, Ragavendiran Padmanaban, and Gayathri

Devi for holding me together. With you all by my side, even the fiercest battles appear like child's play.

All credits for grammar should go to this team that claims to have mastered Wren and Martin: Rangashree Kumar, Priyanka Krishnan, Dhanya S, Visalini Radhakrishnan, Elakkiya Sugi T, Sowndhariya Lakshmi S, Srinidhee K, Nidarshanaa R K, Sutharsha Rajaprakash, Padmapriya Shanmuganathan, and Meghna P. Thank you, guys, for being my grammar police!

Above all, I express my gratitude to the 32 stars featured in this book for sharing my belief that their stories can touch and transform lives.

FOREWORD

It is with immense pride and privilege that I pen this foreword for *Wide Awake*, a book that promises to serve as an inspiring beacon for aspiring Chartered Accountants and students from various professional streams.

The concept of being *Wide Awake*, derived from the Upanishadic verse *Ya esa suptesu jagarti*, encapsulates the essence of perseverance, resilience, and the pursuit of purpose. This book beautifully brings this philosophy to life by chronicling the journeys of 32 exemplary Chartered Accountants who have not only excelled in their fields but have also demonstrated unwavering dedication and hard work in their pursuit of greatness.

Through its compelling narratives and insightful snippets, *Wide Awake* not only motivates but also educates its readers. It offers a treasure trove of practical wisdom and actionable strategies, making it a valuable guide for CA aspirants and professionals alike. It serves as a reminder that success is not merely about reaching a destination but about staying awake and alert to opportunities, even in the face of challenges.

The stories featured in this book stand as a testament to the indomitable human spirit. They reinforce the idea that while the world may rest, those who are *awake*—those who are focused and determined—rise above mediocrity to carve their unique paths.

I commend P. Shandip Sabapathy for his dedication in bringing this project to life. His effort to compile such diverse and powerful accounts is nothing short of remarkable. This book is not just a collection of stories; it is a movement—one that will inspire countless individuals to strive for excellence and believe in their dreams.

It is my hope that *Wide Awake* ignites a spark in the hearts of its readers, encouraging them to embrace life's challenges with courage and determination. May this book serve as a reminder that with persistence, focus, and the right mindset, any goal is attainable.

Wishing every reader an enlightening and transformative journey through these pages.

Warm regards,
Shantha Kalingarayar M.A., B.Ed.,
Correspondent
Vishwa Sishya Vidyodaya School
Bharatiya Vidya Mandir Matric Hr. Sec. School

FOREWORD

We all wish life came with a manual, don't we? One that helps us navigate the challenges that follow us along the journey. But I just realized that while we can search high and low for instructions, in the end, it is always an experience close to us that becomes our guiding light.

Authoring a book might have seemed like a simpler task if someone had given us a step-by-step guide of dos and don'ts. But I truly understood the essence of the process—a herculean task—only through experience. Specifically, the experience of sitting beside the author of this very book, watching him embark on the roller-coaster ride of penning a work brimming with insights.

This book brings together many inspiring stories shared by aspirants who have secured All India Ranks in one of the toughest exams in the country—the Chartered Accountancy Examinations—as well as wisdom imparted by senior members and accomplished leaders of the CA community.

I am a staunch believer in the idea that there is one God, revered by a thousand names. In a similar sense, the Indian education system administers a variety of tests, yet the fundamental approach to preparation remains the same—rooted in sincere effort and consistency. I am extremely glad that this book stands as a testament to my conviction.

A quote I came across that aptly fits this book is: *Flowers are inherently beautiful, but when nurtured with love, they bloom brighter.* Similarly, the stories of each individual compiled in this book are, in their own essence, wonderful and inspiring. The author's magic with words has only enhanced their significance.

When the Superstar of Indian Cinema, Mr. Rajinikanth, was honored as one of NDTV's 25 *Greatest Living Legends* in 2013, his first words were, *"Many people don't believe in miracles, but miracles do happen."* Had someone told me in 2013 that I would be writing the foreword of a book in 2025, I would have laughed. Yet today, I stand as a witness to miracles. And in my story, that miracle is Mr. Shandip Sabapathy.

As I pen this foreword, I take a fond walk down memory lane, reminiscing gratefully about all the acts of positivity and kindness he has bestowed upon me. As an enthusiastic educator and a man who has made it his life's purpose to inspire others through his words, this book is yet another milestone in his endless mission to enrich the lives of those around him.

And after years of preparation, months of writing, and weeks of proofreading, today, the long-awaited moment has finally arrived. His brainchild—a boon we have eagerly anticipated—is here for us to read.

This is a book from the CA fraternity, but not just for the CA fraternity. We believe it will shine as a beacon of hope for aspirants, students, professionals, and many others alike.

From us to you,
Let us all strive to succeed.
Happy reading!

With Love,
CA. M. MAALAN BHARATHI
From the School of P. Shandip Sabapathy

START WITH WHY

Why I wrote this book:

Four inspiring Chartered Accountants—one All India Rank 1 holder and three individuals who had qualified as CAs despite physical disabilities—stood on the grand stage of the National Conference for CA students in Coimbatore. The audience was so awed by their inspiring journeys and personalities that they erupted into a long and thunderous standing ovation!

In that fleeting moment of absolute silence after the applause, a terrible fear gripped my mind. I couldn't reconcile with the thought that the stories of these four remarkable individuals might fade away within the confines of that auditorium. I couldn't bear the idea that all my dear student friends who had missed the conference had also missed the opportunity to be inspired and transformed. As an unwavering believer in the power of stories, I strongly felt that these stories needed to be preserved for posterity.

My father had always nudged (or rather compelled) me to write a book. _"Having a skill and not using it for the welfare of those around you is a sin!"_ he would say, and my mother would nod in agreement. Ever since, I had the desire to write a book—but as it turns out, desire alone isn't enough. The national-level student conference finally gave me a **reason**!

"When you start with WHY, those who believe in what you believe are drawn to you for very personal reasons," said Simon Sinek. True to his words, as soon as I put out a post on social media requesting connections with Chartered Accountancy rank-holders and inspiring CAs, my dear student friends sprang into action! My inbox was flooded with contacts of rank holders and accomplished Chartered Accountants. But they didn't stop at sharing contacts—they also convinced these individuals to grant me interviews!

This book would not have been possible without the love, support, and trust of all those student friends, and for that, I shall always remain indebted.

Why the Title:

In 1949, a group of learned Chartered Accountants requested the great freedom fighter and spiritual master Sri Aurobindo Gosh to suggest a motto and emblem for the Institute of Chartered Accountants of India. Sri Aurobindo chose the Upanishadic verse "Ya Esa Suptesu Jagarti" as the motto. It means "Those who are awake amidst those who are asleep."

True to that Upanishadic verse, the inspiring people featured in this book are those who stayed wide awake, relentlessly pursuing their purpose while those around them slept through life's pleasures—hence the title "Wide Awake."

Shri Aurobindo also suggested the Garuda, or eagle, as the emblem of ICAI because the eagle symbolises qualities like strength, fearlessness, vigilance, and wisdom. The eagle on the cover page is my way of saluting the stars featured in this book for embodying the virtues of the Garuda.

Why You Should Read This Book:

One seed is enough to create a forest;
one spark is enough to cause a forest fire;
and one story is enough to transform your life!

This book isn't really about scoring a rank—it's about becoming the person who deserves a rank. The journeys captured in this book will not only inspire you toward greatness but also guide you there.

If you spend enough time on a train, you'll begin to smell like the train. If you spend enough time in a rose garden, you'll begin smelling like roses. It is my fond hope that if you spend enough time with the stories of these great people, you'll begin smelling of greatness too!

SOME IMPORTANT POINTERS

1. The chapters are arranged neither chronologically nor in order of importance. Every chapter is equally important, and each contains a treasure trove of wisdom. They have been arranged in a manner that provides you, the reader, with a wholesome experience. For your first read, I'd recommend reading the book in the order presented. Thereafter, you can read any chapter at random.

2. Throughout the book, the words of the featured individuals—and even their direct conversations—are presented in italics.

3. The approaches and study methods of the rank-holders vary greatly—and are at times even contradictory. I wanted to lay it all before you so that you can pick what appeals to you.

4. Most of these inspiring personalities are on LinkedIn or Instagram, so you can connect with them via these social media platforms. If you want to write to them, you can email shandipwrites@gmail.com, and we'll forward your message to the respective person.

TABLE OF CONTENTS

THE GOLDEN EAGLE!

CA. T. N. Manoharan

Inspiring CA

Profession brings glory to people, but a select few bring glory to their profession—like Dr. A. P. J. Abdul Kalam, Ratan Tata, Sachin Tendulkar, A. R. Rahman, and CA T. N. Manoharan!

CA T. N. Manoharan, fondly known as TNM Sir in the Chartered Accountant fraternity, is the son of a freedom fighter and farmer, Sri T. L. Narayanasamy Chowdhry. TNM Sir attributes much of his value system to his father, a man of impeccable values and an indomitable spirit!

Sri T. L. Narayanasamy Chowdhry fought for India's independence, initially treading the path of Mahatma Gandhi and seamlessly switching lanes to Subhas Chandra Bose's ideology when needed! TNM Sir fondly recalls:

"Arrests were a natural consequence of his hunger strikes, disturbing railway lines, and the like. But every arrest only strengthened his grit and resolve to free his country from tyranny! Once independence was achieved, his focus shifted to serving society. He served as the President of our village panchayat for 25 years! During that period, he worked tirelessly on infrastructure, employment, and conflict resolution, among other issues. I've witnessed countless under-the-tree panchayat sessions—the kind you now see in movies. My father gave the final verdict, and no one ever challenged it. What amazed me was that both parties would walk away feeling they had received justice! He impacted countless lives along the way. The enormous crowd that gathered for his funeral was a testament to the kind of leader he was!"

The fact that he was unanimously elected for five consecutive terms speaks volumes about the love, respect, and trust he had earned through his impeccable character!

As the saying goes, *"An apple never falls far from the tree."* CA T. N. Manoharan is a glorious extension of the legacy left behind by his remarkable father!

After completing his Bachelor's and Master's in Commerce, he pursued Chartered Accountancy from the Institute of Chartered Accountants of India and later obtained a Law degree from Madras Law College, India.

T. N. Manoharan Sir's life can be summed up in three words: Learn – Earn – Return! He invested his formative years in building a strong academic foundation, then built a successful professional empire, and all along, used his stature and fortune to empower people. His classes and books were free for those who couldn't afford them—and I personally know countless people who have been beneficiaries of his kindness and altruism.

TNM Sir is a rare leader who chose leadership not for stature, but for service! In his own words:

"I never even dreamt of becoming a council member, let alone the President of ICAI! Right from my student days, I could never remain idle. I actively participated in NCC, sports, cultural events—you name it! In college, I signed up for every competition, be it sports, elocution, or cultural events."

After qualifying as a *Chartered Accountant*, he kept himself occupied with three key activities:

1.   Attending seminars, learning, and practicing the profession.

2.   After five years—when he had gained knowledge and maturity—he began presenting papers at seminars, delivering keynote speeches, and more.

3.   Teaching CA students.

These three engagements complemented each other. Before each CA examination, he would select rural centers, camp there for three days, and conduct crash courses on taxation—all for free!

This was a blessing for rural students who lacked access to subject-wise classes. Not only did he teach for free, but he never even claimed reimbursements for his expenses! But then again, what else could you expect from the son of Sri T. L. Narayanasamy Chowdhry?

"Whenever I visited rural branches, I was used to hearing student grievances—'I didn't even get a response to my correspondence!', 'This reform would be beneficial', 'This could be executed better'—and all these concerns stayed with me. Eventually, I thought, Why remain a mere spectator? Why not go to the helm of affairs and make a difference? So I went to my village, sought my parents' blessings, and filed my nomination for the Central Council."

In his very first election, CA T. N. Manoharan won with 1,735 votes—the highest vote count at the time! He was the only candidate declared elected in the first round. After serving on the Council for five years, he became the President of ICAI in 2006.

Remember the complaint students made about not receiving responses to their letters?

As ICAI President, TNM Sir personally ensured that every single mail addressed to him was answered! To manage this along with his hectic travel and work schedule was no easy task.

"I never saw the sunrise in Delhi! Whenever I wasn't traveling, I'd leave the office between 1 a.m. and 3 a.m. and return at 9 a.m. sharp. Not a single email remained unanswered! Even today, I have copies of all that correspondence stored in box files."

After his tenure as ICAI President, at the age of 50, he stepped back from meeting clients, choosing instead to focus all his time and energy on serving the nation.

What about family, I wonder aloud. His face beams with pride as he says, *"Both my daughters, Malavika Varun and Sahini Krishna, are practicing Chartered Accountants, following in my footsteps!"*

On January 7, 2009, a ₹5,000 crore fraud rocked Satyam Computer Services Ltd. Stock prices plummeted, millions of lives (employees, investors, customers) were impacted, and—above all—India's global reputation was at stake.

The Government of India responded swiftly, forming a six-member crisis management board, which included: Kiran Karnik, CA Deepak Parekh, Tarun Das, Late Shri C. Achuthan (Shandip's mentor), Balakrishna Mainak and CA. T. N. Manoharan.

One member had to stay full-time in Hyderabad to oversee the revival. TNM Sir volunteered.

His only request?

"Since we are doing this for our country, we should not accept any compensation for this assignment—no matter how long it takes!"

In just 100 days—what should have taken four years—the board revived Satyam and facilitated its takeover by Tech Mahindra.

For his extraordinary service, TNM Sir's name was unanimously recommended for the Padma Shri—without his knowledge!

Though he had received numerous accolades—NDTV's Business Leadership Award, CNN IBN's Indian of the Year, and multiple Lifetime Achievement Awards—the Padma Shri was special. It was Mother India's pat on her child's back for saving her reputation!

But when I ask how he felt, his response shocks me.

"I was upset and angry!"

Seeing my confusion, he clarifies:

"I felt I was just doing my duty. Why should the government feel the need to reward me? But when my entire CA fraternity celebrated it as their success, I felt satisfied. And I was deeply grateful to the government for bestowing such immense joy upon my parents."

On the day TNM Sir walked the red carpet to receive the Padma Shri, his mother and wife cheered him on in the Rashtrapati Bhavan, while his father—who had lost his vision—listened from home, a tear rolling down his cheek.

Life had come full circle.

Garuda, the Golden Eagle, is our emblem.

And TNM, the Golden Eagle, is our pride!

A SPARK IS ENOUGH!

CA. Madhumitha

AIR 27 – Final – Nov 2022

"I found a spark, which I placed in the hollow of a tree, and the spark consumed the entire forest!" wrote poet Subramaniya Bharathi. Bharathi is the thread that connects Madhumitha and me!

Every once in a while, I'd get a random call or message from her saying, *"Sir, please recite that inspiring poem by Bharathi—I want to hear it in your voice!"* If I am Bharathi's voice to her, she is Bharathi's definition of an iron lady to me!

Here's a related party disclosure: I've been a close witness to her inspiring journey to the top; I had the blessed fortune of mentoring Madhumitha for her CA Final examinations.

One morning, out of the blue, I got a call inviting me to a felicitation program organized by a private CA coaching academy. The voice on the other side said, *"Sir, one of our students who scored 62 in Law and*

90s in other papers attributes her success to your motivational talk at our academy! So, it would be great if you could come and felicitate her." It was at that function that Madhumitha shared her journey with me:

"Sir, I endured a hectic schedule in college and CA classes for a year. Just when I had completed my Group 1 Intermediate syllabus, I met with an accident while returning from a test at the academy. Everything came to a grinding halt—I couldn't even do basic chores, and I slipped into depression.

One day, CA Arjun Rao Sir called me and compelled me to attend a talk at our academy on 'How to Ace CA Exams.' Your talk was like therapy to me! I had decided not to appear for the exams in that attempt, but inspired by your words, I resumed my preparations and ended up scoring these marks. That's why Arjun Sir insisted that you be the one to felicitate me."

Pro-tip: *A single spark can consume a mighty forest. A single spark can change your life! The trick is to take that spark and carefully nurture it in the depths of your heart so that it consumes you.*

Madhumitha then completed Group 2 in the subsequent attempt and entered the CA Final arena. *"I completed classes for three papers during my articleship—over a span of one year. By the end of April, I was done with all the classes!"*

Pro-tip: *Notice how almost every rank holder gets an unbeatable edge by beginning early.*

"What are the factors that helped you keep the spark alive?" I ask. After a childlike laugh, she replies:

"Sir, these are things you taught me through mentoring. And I'm going to repeat them to you now! Hasn't life come full circle?" Together, we laugh—happy and proud of what we've accomplished!

Then came the three sparks of inspiration:

1. Sunday breaks: Not taking breaks will wear us out quickly.

2. Measuring study hours & progress: Tracking study time and daily progress was a game-changer.

3. Breaking down big milestones: Dividing larger goals into smaller daily tasks reduced stress.

No matter how well you prepare, low days are inevitable—even for rank holders! Here's how Madhumitha handled them:

"My mother played a pivotal role in helping me sail through emotional storms. And on low days, I'd tell myself, 'A little more effort may give an All India Rank, so increase your efforts!'"

What exactly was the effort? What were Madhumitha's study methods?

1. Following a written schedule.

2. Striking out/eliminating portions I'd never revisit. This saved a lot of time.

3. Using 30-minute slots for challenging portions.

After a chuckle, Madhumitha adds, *"Sir, on the first day of my Auditing preparation, I called you in a panic, crying that I couldn't relate to the Standards of Audit and Professional Ethics—I was completely clueless about what to do. And you asked me to confine them to 30-minute slots interspersed with other subject slots. That helped me cruise through the Auditing paper without losing my sanity."*

"Sir, the greatest challenge in the CA preparation journey is handling emotions, and that's where mentoring was a boon for me! I'd strongly advise students to create a support system that can bolster them, handhold them, and help them navigate these emotional storms."

I completely agree with Madhumitha—handling emotions is one of the greatest challenges, and emotional support is a necessity, not a luxury.

"Now that we've discussed challenges, can you talk about mistakes—the most common ones?" I nudge.

Madhumitha shares two common mistakes most students commit:

1. Lack of consistency.

2. Aiming for 40 or 50—the bare minimum marks.

She then speaks animatedly about an All India Rank:

"Awareness about ranks is quite low in South India. Here, we often believe that simply qualifying as a CA is enough. But in the northern parts of the country, they see a rank as a ticket to bigger opportunities.

And please make noise about this, Sir! Rank holders are entitled to a Management Development Programme, where we get to learn from eminent faculties at IIM or ISB. Spending 15 days with 49 other AIR holders is such an amazing experience!"

"What happens when 50 rank holders meet?" I ask out of curiosity.

With childlike enthusiasm, Madhumitha says, *"At first, we assume that everyone except ourselves is a genius. But other than a handful of people, everyone is ordinary—confident and insecure in equal measures, childlike, fun-loving, optimistic, and so on. We walked around the majestic campus of IIM, made good friends, and had loads of fun."*

I am now interested in knowing the three life lessons Madhumitha learned on her journey toward a rank:

1. I learned the importance of consistency.

2. I learned the importance of family.

3. I learned that striving to make others happy is a greater driving force than striving for our own happiness. The thought that I shouldn't let Arjun Rao Sir and Shandip Sir down made me push harder each day.

Madhumitha is now soaring high in the corporate skies of the Aditya Birla Group. Her accomplishments shine bright, but even brighter is the spark of goodness in her!

Dear reader,

I wish and pray that someday, you too will cross paths with Madhumitha—so that her spark of goodness may inspire and uplift you! As for me, I shall await her call saying, *"Sir, please recite that inspiring poem by Bharathi—I want to hear it in your voice!"*

<u>Choose Wisely</u>

Krishna was Arjuna's mentor,

Shakuni was Dhuryodhana's mentor,

And this made all the difference in their lives!

So, please choose your principal, teachers, and mentors wisely.

THE SCIENCE GUY

CA. H. Shashank Karthick

AIR 37 – CA Final – Dec 2021

"I didn't like science, so I chose commerce and I landed in CA," was the most repeated response when I asked how these rank-holders got into CA. I am truly blown away when Shashank says, *"I'm a science guy; I wanted to be a research scientist. I was even a district topper in IIT coaching! My friends' parents were CAs, so my friends chose CA; thanks to their influence, I chose CA."*

"I'm a very mathematical person; I'm a science guy!" he repeats, throwing a statistic at me as if to substantiate it: 10 of his college classmates plunged into CA, 9 qualified, 3 of them scored a rank, and 7 qualified on the first attempt.

Takeaway: *Consciously surround yourself with people who are as driven and committed as you are. Flying as a flock is always easier, provided you are headed in the same direction.*

So, did he expect a rank? *"I knew I'd get a rank (he didn't say I believed; he said: I KNEW). I didn't even check my marks; I only checked the merit list!"*

Such confidence can only come from extraordinary effort. So where did those efforts come from? *"I strive to be the best at what I do,"* he says with calm confidence.

If Shashank were a brand, his tagline would be: *"I came, I saw, I conquered!"*

He learned about the Aditya Birla Group Leadership Program through a YouTube channel and decided that he was getting into the Aditya Birla Group (ABG). Since ABG hires only All India rank holders and MBA graduates from Tier 1 colleges in their flagship ABGLP program, Shashank decided to score a rank!

"To score a rank: 100% clarity about the syllabus, exams, valuation, and the like is a must. So, I reached out to rank holders via LinkedIn, and their inputs proved valuable in this regard."

Champions in every field share one common trait: reaching out. They, too, have all the inhibitions we do—even the fear of appearing stupid— but their aspirations drive them to rise above their shortcomings. That's precisely why aspirations are important.

Also, if you are aspiring to a remarkable career, Shashank advises you to take your articleship seriously. *"Articleship is as important as studies. With regard to studies, it is all about conversion—converting your preparation into a precise answer in the examination,"* he says.

According to him, conversion is a three-step process:

1. Revise
2. Recall
3. Reproduce

The science guy that he is, he has researched study strategies and preparation methods like no one ever has. His knowledge in this regard is truly mind-blowing!

Here are 7 pointers from the man himself:

1. Getting the basics right:

Learn to:

    a)   Prepare honestly,

    b)   Breathe correctly, and

    c)   Sleep deeply.

If you can master these three, you can become a champion in any field!

"Someone who can't sleep right or breathe right can't focus properly."

2. Measurement and momentum:

Only what gets measured gets accomplished. Race against yourself—your next lap should always be faster than the previous one.

On the index page, note down how much time you take to study a chapter. The next time you revise, you shouldn't take more than 50% of the previous time. This metric is an acid test to determine if your last study or revision was effective. It also gives you clarity on how much time you'll need for each chapter during those crucial 1.5 days between exams. Your target is to condense a 60–65 marks syllabus into 10 hours of study.

3. Retain and recall:

End every day with a win! You already know which concepts you might forget. Keep a diary. As you study, write down the names of the concepts you think you are likely to forget. Before winding down at night, review the list and see if you can recall the concepts. *"You don't have to say them out loud; if you're honest with yourself, you'll know the moment you see the topic."* Tick off all the concepts you can recall and quickly review the ones you can't. Repeat this exercise the next morning.

4. Mistakes:

Never repeat mistakes! Simply avoiding them can earn you an extra 10–20 marks on each paper.

Every time you make a mistake—or even think you might make one in any concept—go back to the main textbook and note the mistake, along with the correction, next to the concept. This practice helps you create a *"checklist of errors to avoid"* for each concept. You should be able to review your list of mistakes on the day of your exam.

5. Taking notes:

For each topic, compile your learnings from multiple sources into one set of notes. Take notes only where they can replace the book; you shouldn't need the book again. Your notes are effective only if they save you time without compromising quality. Eliminate unnecessary details. Don't keep revising what you're already confident about—you don't have the luxury of time for reassurance.

6. Presentation:

Don't obsess over presentation in the exams! It's similar to school exams, and you are experienced enough by now. Instead, focus on concept clarity and accurately reproducing answers.

7. Mock tests:

A mock test a day keeps exam fear away!

Mock tests are meant to assess your thinking, not your presentation skills.

An exam has two parts: the process of deciding what to write and the actual writing. You should be able to complete the thinking part in less than an hour, leaving you two hours to write as fast and as comprehensively as possible. During mock tests, focus on the thinking part by writing down core concepts on the question paper itself. Allocate 1 hour for the test, 15 minutes for evaluation, and 15 minutes to note down mistakes and corrections.

He has already shared so much, but I'm greedy for more! So I ask, *"If there's only one piece of advice you can give students, what would it be?"* His response is absolutely profound: *"To succeed, integrity is very important. Most people are so scared of their own ineffectiveness that they don't want to track themselves."* Being ruthlessly honest with ourselves (without beating ourselves up) is an art we must master if we want to attain greatness.

So how did Shashank handle low days without beating himself up? *"I'd simply remind myself that there's no time for thinking, only time for doing!"*

Conversing with Shashank is like watching a Rajinikanth movie—nothing is impossible, every statement is a punchline, and the energy is absolutely contagious!

Another All India rank holder told me, *"I was not even headed towards a rank. Two months before my exams, I called Shashank to discuss something, and that one phone call changed everything! Shashank has that effect on people!"* When I asked yet another rank holder why he had agreed to contribute to this book, he said, *"I had Shashank; I want this book to be there for those who don't have a Shashank in their lives!"*

Scoring a rank is heroic; empowering others to do so is legendary!

May Shashank continue to spread his magic, and may this book create magic too—the Shashank way!

I HAVE A DREAM!

CA. G. Ramasamy

Inspiring CA

In 1984, a youngster hailing from a humble agricultural family qualified as a Chartered Accountant and received his certificate of membership from the Institute of Chartered Accountants of India. Even as he stood admiring his certificate with tear-filled eyes, he noticed a signature on it with the words "President, ICAI" beneath. At that very moment, he announced to his friends, "Someday I will become the President of ICAI and sign other people's certificates!" How's that for the audacity of hope?

CA G. Ramasamy's dream was to become a doctor, but destiny had other plans for him! When he couldn't get into any medical college, an acquaintance told him that Chartered Accountancy had a bright future since Coimbatore was swiftly growing as an industrial hub. And so he took the plunge! Interestingly, CA Day and Doctors' Day are both celebrated on the same day—the 1st of July.

His CA preparation journey was by no means easy! *"There were no coaching classes back then, and self-study was the only option. And hailing from a Tamil-medium background made things worse for me. I spent 2 hours each day with a friend who taught me how to understand the language, how to present, and so on."*

"After putting in so much effort, didn't it hurt to fail?" I ask, fearing that my question might sound silly to him. One of his noble attributes is that he'd never make you feel small!

"Failure meant I lacked something; I discovered what that was, strengthened those weak links, and the results had to come!"

He even completed CS alongside CA!

After qualifying as a Chartered Accountant, he experienced the same insecurity that any newly qualified CA from a humble background would have: *"Do I have it in me to set up my own office and succeed?"*

He approached one of his mentors, who advised him to attend seminars, interact with a lot of people, and involve himself in the activities of the Coimbatore Branch of the Institute of Chartered Accountants of India. Thus began his political stint.

"The past-president GR" that we look up to in awe is only the tip of an enormous iceberg! Beneath that tip lie countless years of untiring effort and failures. CA G. Ramasamy lost his first election by a thin margin, and he did just what he had done as a CA student: he identified and strengthened his weak links!

"I worked harder, networked extensively, discovered their challenges and expectations, learned which competencies I lacked and worked on them, and the results had to come! I won the subsequent election and became a member of the Central Council!"

Going to Delhi to attend council meetings meant waking up at 2 a.m. to board the 3:30 a.m. flight to Chennai so that he could catch the Delhi flight from there! At the committee meetings, any member who wanted to make a point would display his or her name on a board, and the President would give them an opportunity to voice their views. CA G. Ramasamy worked incredibly hard to prepare for those meetings, and whenever he got an opportunity, he made a good impression by voicing his views eloquently and convincingly. The goodwill he earned landed him opportunities to work on various committees.

And in 2011, that youngster who had vowed to become the President of ICAI someday finally ascended the throne. It took him 27 years of relentless effort to achieve his dreams! It is no wonder, then, that he begins every speech with Swami Vivekananda's quote, "Arise, awake, and stop not till the goal is reached!"

Some of his accomplishments as President are:

1. Preparing the Vision 2030 document.
2. Initiating and establishing regular interactions with CAs in public service.
3. Allowing 15 minutes of reading time for students in the CA exams.

By now, I am curious to know the skills that helped him become the President of ICAI, and he names three skills:

1. Listening: Agreeing or disagreeing is secondary—you have to listen!
2. Not getting worked up when things don't go your way.
3. Remaining humble: People will praise us out of love and respect, but we shouldn't let any of it go to our heads!

"And what were your three daily habits?" I ask curiously. *"Before WhatsApp or after WhatsApp?"* he asks, laughing heartily.

Meanwhile, coffee is served, and he personally removes our empty cups from the table. As I sit there, staring at him in awe, I wonder how someone could remain untouched and unchanged by power, fame, and glory! To me, he is "GR Uncle"—my father's friend who qualified as a CA alongside my father. And as someone who has known him for over three decades, I can vouch for the fact that he has not let fame or success change him one wee bit!

Clearing his throat, he continues:

Pre-WhatsApp:

1. Reading the newspaper.
2. Walking or golfing.
3. Reading professional content.

Post-WhatsApp:

1. Reading and responding to all the WhatsApp messages he receives (most of them are from people seeking his opinion or advice on important matters).
2. Reading the newspaper.
3. Walking or golfing.

What remains unchanged in both the pre – and post-WhatsApp eras is his habit of rising early and making the most out of his mornings.

What amazes me is that politics usually means you make more enemies than friends, but not GR; he's the Dale Carnegie of the CA fraternity! So I ask him for some pointers on winning friends and influencing people.

I'll tell you what I follow:

1. Contradict politely. You can always agree to disagree—but do it respectfully.
2. Treat everyone as your kith and kin—as the Tamil poet Kaniyan Poongundran wrote.
3. Be open to feedback.

"Feedback is okay, but how did you handle unreasonable criticism and unpleasant people?" I ask. With a sagely smile, he says, *"Handle both of them with grace."*

Such wisdom can only come from decades of experience and countless hours of introspection! Wanting to carefully pass on some of that wisdom to posterity, I ask him for some words of advice for CA aspirants and novices:

1. Chart a roadmap for your career. If you don't know where you want to go, you'll end up going to the wrong place.

2. Continuing professional education is absolutely important: attend seminars, pursue certification, and invest time each day in learning.

3. Specialization is important. Pick an area and strive to become an expert.

Having accomplished so much, having seen it all, I wonder what drives him now. After a hearty laugh, he says, "I still have so much more to learn! What is known is a handful; the unknown is an ocean!"

"Most leaders are readers; how about you?" I ask curiously.

"I love books!" he says, and names three of his favorites:

1. Parthiban Kanavu (a classic Tamil novel)

2. The Power of Positive Thinking by Norman Vincent Peale

3. How to Get Whatever You Want by Kop Mayer

He continues:

"But please remember that practicing is as important as reading. That's actually the whole point of reading. I used to sincerely apply whatever I learned from all those self-help books. I used to stand in front of the mirror and tell myself, 'GR, you are great!' My wife would laugh at me, saying, 'How humble of you!' And I'd reply with a smile, 'I'm only telling GR that he's great—I'm not telling others.'"

It seems that Bernard Berenson was right after all when he said, *"Miracles happen to those who believe in them!"*

GR, you are really great!

<u>Do You See It?</u>

Walt Disney's brother Roy Disney made Walt's dream of 'Disneyland' come true after Walt's demise. At the opening ceremony of Disneyland, a journalist asked Roy, "Are you sad that Walt Disney passed away before seeing Disneyland?"

Roy's instant reply was, "We wouldn't be standing here if Walt hadn't already seen it!"

Success happens twice: first on the inside, and then on the outside.

DECIDE, COMMIT, SUCCEED!

Ms. Dharsa Vikashini

AIR 32 – CA Foundation – Nov 2019

If you can say, *"They believed in me even before I believed in myself!"* then you are immensely blessed! Dharsa was fortunate to have a tuition teacher who believed that she was an ideal candidate for Chartered Accountancy. Thus began the fairy tale.

"I've always had the understanding that educational qualification is the true asset—and I wanted to make my parents proud!"

This is one common factor I noticed among many rank holders: they tied their goal to a cause bigger than personal wealth or glory. Wanting to repay your parents for all their countless sacrifices is indeed a powerful driving force!

Optimism plays an undeniable role in success! Dharsa is bubbling with energy when she says, *"My faculty once said, 'There will be 5 All India*

Rank Holders from this batch,' and I strongly believed that I was one of them!" Only if you can dream it, can you accomplish it!

Contrary to popular belief, success doesn't come from doing extraordinary things; it comes from doing ordinary things with extraordinary consistency. And that is precisely what Dharsa did.

Here are 3 simple strategies that got Dharsa an AIR:

1. 7–8 hours of quality sleep that kept me brisk throughout the day.

2. Early morning studies: I'd begin my studies at 6 a.m. on the terrace, amidst nature—in the company of birds, squirrels, peacocks, and pigeons. Studying in that ambience kept me fresh.

3. Smart work: I prepared notes and charts, and studied from them instead of going back to the textbook for revisions. This saved a lot of time while improving my efficiency.

"But that extraordinary consistency doesn't come easy, right? How did you achieve it?" I ask curiously.

Dharsa replies immediately, *"Success demands sacrifices, sir! I didn't have a social life at all at that time. I didn't even use a smartphone—I used a button phone to cut off distractions."* This reminds me of a quote that says, *"If you want to live the life that only 1% of people live, you should be willing to do what only 1% of people are willing to do!"*

With a bit of hesitation, I ask, *"You got so many aspects right—which is why you scored an AIR—but mistakes are unavoidable, right? So, what was one mistake that you made in your preparation journey?"*

Dharsa doesn't hesitate one bit: *"I should have taken up classes for Auditing. I scored only 48 because I did self-study."*

Disclaimer: Please don't interpret the above as meaning that classes or coaching are mandatory! Time will always be your key factor; so unless you begin very early, you will not have time for classes in all subjects. You don't need them either—you need to decide solely based on your strengths and weaknesses.

Whether you take classes or not, one inevitable challenge you will face in your preparation journey is the occasional emotional low. (This applies to every journey or endeavor in life.) And how you handle those lows will decide how high you go.

"The emotional videos of successful CA results on YouTube kept me going! I also pasted a printout of CA Natarajan's results and a newspaper clipping of CA Lakshmanan Arasu being honoured to keep myself inspired!" (Both of these people are featured in this book.)

One common pitfall Dharsa wants CA students to avoid is aiming for 40 or 50—the bare minimum marks. *"Please aim high; avoid mediocrity."* In other words, aim for the moon—even if you miss, you may hit a star!

"Thank you so much for your time. I have one last question: Where do you see yourself 10 years from now?" I ask curiously. Dharsa's instant reply is, *"Family and teaching! I love teaching; I'd balance family and teaching."*

I can see Dharsa standing tall amidst a class of 100 students, passionately declaring, *"There will be 5 All India Rank Holders from this batch!"*

I CAN!

CA. Essakiraj Arumugam

AIR 1 – CA Final – Nov 2020

Can you score an All India Rank without even aspiring for one?
Yes, you can!

Can you score a rank even if you didn't study in an English-medium school?
Yes, you can!

Can you score an AIR in CA Final even if you couldn't achieve it in Foundation or Intermediate?
Yes, you can!

Can you have an AIR 1 on your profile and yet have no air about you?
Yes, you can!

"Yes, you can!" is the answer to every single question or self-doubt you have—if, like Essakiraj, you believe from the bottom of your heart: *"I can!"*

Essakiraj is just one of countless students who chose commerce because he didn't like science and then plunged into CA because it was one of the best options available to a commerce student. But he is one of those rare individuals who transitioned from Tamil medium to English medium in the 11th standard.

"What my peers did 1–2 times, I had to do 5–6 times, thanks to my lack of English knowledge! My father helped me by teaching sentence structuring using The Hindu newspaper."

Imagine having to learn the basics of English while also keeping up with the intense academic pressure of 11th and 12th standard—tests, portions, special classes. Add to that the feeling of being the odd one out in a new school! Handling all this as a teenager is tough. Incredibly tough. Tough—but not impossible!

Well, nothing is impossible if you are Essakiraj.

Nothing is impossible if you truly believe, *"I can!"*

"A lot of people discouraged me, saying CA is too tough and that I was taking a huge risk. But I didn't listen to the negativity because I was confident about my efforts!"

Essakiraj had to postpone his IPCC exams because the syllabus was vast, and his Tamil-medium background made comprehension difficult.

"After 5.5 months of classes and 6–7 months of self-study, I passed my IPCC exams—but with mediocre marks because I had made a lot of mistakes in my preparation!"

Like you, I was curious too! What were those mistakes?

1. Not knowing how to approach a subject.

2. Not being aware of my own strengths and weaknesses.

3. Not estimating the time required for preparation, leading to poor study planning.

4. Failing to assess the quality of my study—how much of the concepts I actually retained.

5. Not knowing how to study effectively—balancing speed with quality.

"I firmly decided not to repeat these mistakes in CA Final," says Essakiraj.

"The day you decide to turn your life around is the day your life turns around!" I note down.

After six months of classes and six months of self-study, Essakiraj was all set for the May 2020 exams. But then, the exams got postponed—thanks to COVID.

"And you still scored AIR 1 despite that?" I ask in disbelief.

After a classic Essakiraj smile comes the classic Essakiraj modesty:

"Well, the exams were finally held in November 2020. So I got six extra months—which meant extra revisions, extra mock tests, and I could also cover the portions I had skipped before."

As someone who has been mentoring CA aspirants since 2015, I can vouch that 2020 was the most challenging year. COVID and the lockdown turned everything upside down. Classes came to a sudden halt, academies struggled to transition to virtual learning, students were confined to their homes, and many had loved ones affected by COVID.

Worse, the exam dates were completely uncertain.

I personally know many talented students—potential rank holders—who failed because they got caught up in the noise of uncertainty. Social media was abuzz with speculation about whether exams would even happen.

So, how did Essakiraj handle the uncertainty?

"Anyway, the exam has to happen someday. My preparedness alone is what matters! I told myself: 'If exams happen tomorrow, I should be able to write well.' I always expect the worst and prepare myself to handle it!"

"Your surroundings matter too. Avoid people who spread negativity. That is their conditioning—we needn't get caught up in it!"

I noticed this common trait among all achievers: When things turn chaotic, they turn on noise-cancellation mode and dive into their work with laser focus.

The beauty of this journey is that Essakiraj never aimed for a rank!

"I just wanted to give my best since this was going to be the last exam of my academic life! I never studied concepts just for marks—my focus was always on mastering each concept."

Take care of the process, and the results will follow automatically.

So, what was the process like for Essakiraj? What did he do to achieve AIR 1?

1. Have a solid daily plan and focus on completing that day's portions rather than obsessing over study hours.

2. Recall the day's portions before going to bed.

3. Learn by teaching others.

4. Use mnemonics, stories, and visualization techniques to retain concepts effectively.

5. Forget the "golden number" of three revisions! I did seven revisions for Auditing and three for the rest. Decide based on your grip over the subject.

When asked about the most important traits for success, Essakiraj names three: curiosity, intensity, and being undistractable.

"Mindset is everything! You can always develop a skill set if you have the right mindset."

"Please give my readers one master tip!" I request.

After pondering for a minute, Essakiraj smiles and says, *"I'll give you three!"*

1. We study a lot without practical exposure, making it hard to comprehend and retain concepts. Absorb real-world applications from news and current affairs. This helps in better understanding, retention, and connecting theory to practice.

2. In the real world, knowledge alone doesn't matter—problem-solving does. So, while studying, ask yourself:

    - What problem does this solve?

    - How does this solve the problem?

3. Be creative! Even small acts of creativity can boost performance.

I ask for an example, and he says, *"While solving long sums, I always begin on the left-side page. That way, if it extends beyond one page, I don't have to flip pages!"*

If this interview makes you think Essakiraj must be a warrior, think again!

He is a musician—a devout student of Carnatic music and an ardent fan of Sanjay Subramaniam, a cult figure in Carnatic music who also happens to be a Chartered Accountant!

Even our conversation feels like a beautiful piece of Carnatic music—thanks to his melodious voice, perfect pauses, and soft demeanor.

So many questions whirl in my mind as I finish penning this article:

Can a person remain this humble and unassuming after accomplishing so much?

Can a soft-natured musician thrive in the fierce corporate world?

Can I ever become as pure, kind, and loving as him?

And then, the voice of God echoes from within:

"Yes, you can!"

"I can!" is the answer to every single question or self-doubt you have—if, like Essakiraj, you believe from the bottom of your heart: **"I can!"**

<u>Blessed Are the Believers</u>

Until 1954 it was widely believed that it was humanly impossible to run a mile in less than 4 minutes. Athletes had been chasing this elusive goal since as early as 1886, and even the most gifted runners and most brilliant coaches failed. Some medical journals even reported that it was physiologically impossible for the human body to break this barrier.

However, on May 6 that year, Sir Roger Bannister shattered this barrier by running a mile in just 3 minutes and 59 seconds in Oxford, England. Remarkably, he achieved this fear without any formal coaching.

Even more remarkable was the fact that 3 more runners broke his record in the weeks that followed. Since then, over 1700 athletes have broken the 4 minute mile barrier!

So, the challenge wasn't really physiological but psychological. For your body to accomplish something, your mind must first believe that it can!

Can you write and clear both groups in the 1st attempt?

Can you score above 60 in your challenging papers?

Can you score an All India Rank?

Yes you can, IF you believe that you can!

Blessed are the believers for they allow miracles to happen to them.

THE DIVINE CHARIOTEER

CA. M. P. Vijay Kumar

Inspiring CA

On a cold morning in 2011, as early as 5:30 a.m., over a thousand CA students waded through knee-deep water to reach a majestic auditorium named Mylapore Fine Arts Club. It was in this auditorium that the legendary actor Sivaji Ganesan enacted many of his dramas; it was in this auditorium that the legendary singer Yesudas performed most of his New Year concerts; and it was in this auditorium that the legendary teacher CA M. P. Vijayakumar taught accountancy and law for decades!

Thanks to "Cyclone Laila" — rain that lashed all night — most of Chennai's roads were submerged, and Chennai's transportation system came to a grinding halt! But all of this wasn't good enough to stop over a thousand of us from attending our accountancy classes, courtesy of CA M. P. Vijayakumar, or "MPV Sir," as we fondly called him! Yes, you read that right—a thousand of us! A thousand is a mighty strength for a national-level conference for CA students; and over a thousand was the daily strength of MPV Sir's classes!

It wasn't just his teaching prowess that drew us to him; it was the person he was! To him, we weren't just students; we were his "children!" And to us, he wasn't just a teacher — he was our inspiration! He was who we wanted to be when we qualified CA!

One morning, as he was teaching, the mic made a gushing noise—thanks to a glitch. MPV Sir then requested a student to go out and bring the technician, and the student happily obliged. MPV Sir continued dictating, and we continued writing. When I looked up, I noticed that MPV was missing from the stage, but his voice kept blaring through the speakers! Upon scanning the auditorium, we found him sitting in the seat of the student he had sent, writing notes for that student even as he was dictating! *"I've sent him for my need, and he shouldn't be affected because of that,"* was the thought process!

Since I was a kid, teachers sending students out for chores was an everyday sight. But for the first time in my life, I saw a teacher sit and write notes for the student he had sent! At that moment, I whispered to my friend, *"If I become a teacher someday, I will strive to be at least 1% of this great man!"* It's been a decade since I qualified CA and became a teacher, and the last 10 years of my life have been nothing but a humble attempt to be at least 1% of who MPV Sir is!

This is only my experience. Every student of MPV Sir would have at least one awe-inspiring story of how he touched and transformed their life! That's CA M. P. Vijayakumar for you!

And here is his story:

"Back in the 1980s, the norm was to complete engineering and go abroad—and my family was no different! But thanks to my interest in cricket, I didn't score enough to gain admission to a good engineering

college in my region, so I ended up in B.Com. Much of the society in which I lived looked down upon me and even ostracized me for not getting into engineering. Even my parents were truly concerned, but thanks to my playful attitude, I continued playing cricket and sauntering around without any regret or care!

One evening, as I was returning on my bicycle after a game of cricket, a friend's father called out to me from outside his electrical shop. Other than the fact that his daughter was my classmate at school, I wasn't well acquainted with him at all, so I walked up to him, wondering why he had called me. He was a very imposing man, aggressive in his demeanour. He lashed out at me, saying, "What are you up to in life? These are the crucial years of your life, and you shouldn't be wasting them away like this! There's a course called ICWA (Cost Accounting)—at least pursue that. It will help you settle!"

Even today, I'm clueless about why he stopped me that day and why he cared enough to advise me! He even followed up through his daughter, who told me more than once, "I'm attending ICWA classes, and Dad keeps asking me if you've joined." "Seems like he won't spare me!" I thought to myself, and I enrolled in classes!

Back then, ICWA classes were supported entirely by the Port Trust, and that was a big boon to me! Another blessing was my circle of friends—friends like Mukesh, who was exceptionally intelligent, and Atchut, who was exceptionally hardworking. I borrowed a bit from both and cleared my ICWA Foundation with 68% marks. Buoyed by the confidence this victory gave me, I cleared the Intermediate and Final exams of ICWA in my first attempt!

I was recognized by the Vizag branch of ICWA for having qualified with good marks, and it was there that a teacher named Sri V. S. N. Murthy nudged me to pursue CA. Though I had qualified CWA, I wasn't even aware of CA until Murthy Sir educated me about it that day. His nudge led me to pursue CA.

I sat there wondering if his teacher would have had any clue at all that his gentle whisper would echo across decades and transform countless lives! It was like a lioness teaching a lion cub to see his reflection in water: once you show him who he is, you just can't stop him from ruling the jungle! MPV Sir qualified CS, and he earned his CA with an All India Rank of 50 in Intermediate and AIR 20 in CA Final! And he did all of this by self-study!

A farm may help create a lamb, but only a harsh jungle can create a lion! MPV Sir's path was far from easy:

Both of my friends went to Chennai for classes, but I couldn't afford to go because of our family's economic situation, so I had to study using my friend's notes. I couldn't even afford to photocopy them, so I had to borrow them each day! His house was 8 km away from mine, so my brother would cycle there to bring the notebook for me, saving me from getting tired! I'd study and return the book the next day. And having written the CWA and CS exams equipped me with the much-needed writing skills! All these efforts culminated in an AIR 20 in CA Final!"

Pause for a moment and ponder upon this:

The boy who couldn't go to Chennai for classes inspired countless boys and girls to flock to Chennai for classes! This, my dear friend, is the power of education and hard work! Education is the greatest enabler, and hard work is the biggest game-changer!

Qualifying with a rank opened many doors, and he received offer letters from even mighty companies such as Tata Steel, Indal, etc. But CA M. P. Vijayakumar's life isn't a calculated one! He landed in Sundaram Finance—the same group for which his father had served for countless years! And he's truly glad—and even grateful—about that!

The organization where you begin your career shapes who you are as a professional! The pay package was lower than the other offers I had, but the value systems I acquired from Sundaram Finance are priceless!

And even today, my stint at Sundaram Finance adds so much to my credentials!

Pro-tip: This is also why your choice of principal is extremely important! If you want to become a Vivekananda, you need to find a Ramakrishna— and be a worthy pupil!

MPV Sir's life wasn't a calculated one! He was open to miracles, deserving of miracles, and miracles happened to him—so naturally! Thanks to a nudge from a friend, he began teaching, and it became increasingly difficult to balance a corporate job with teaching. There was also a constant tug at his heart to venture on his own, so he quit his job and plunged into practice!

After a brief stint in practice, he joined Sify Technologies on a short-term engagement. What was intended to be a 100-metre dash turned into a marathon, and to this day, CA M. P. Vijayakumar is the Executive Director and Group CFO of Sify Technologies. He also contested and won the Central Council elections of ICAI in 2016 and served on the council from 2016 to 2022.

MPV Sir has authored over a dozen books on Accounting and Accounting Standards. He has earned countless awards and recognitions, including the "Asia Business Leader of the Year Award 2024," induction into the CFO Hall of Fame by the CFO Collective, and many others. He has accomplished far more than he ever dreamt of! He has reached the pinnacle of success—and he did it with utmost grace and elan! But that's not my sole reason for wanting to write about him!

Many aspire for greatness; some attain it; only a select few drive others to the shore of greatness! They're the divine charioteers carefully picked by the universe to keep the fabric of humanity alive!

Arjunas are plenty; Krishnas are few! And that's why their stories are important! We share them not to glorify the Krishnas, but so that countless Arjunas like you and me may prosper!

When an Arjuna meets a Krishna, questions are only a natural consequence, right?

"Having tasted success in so many spheres and to such a great magnitude, how would you define success now?" I asked.

"It is your ability to be happy by doing what you want to do!" he said with a smile.

What drives him now, I wonder. And he says it is the opportunity to learn and the opportunity to contribute! *"Economics has never driven me! Luxuries are never an incentive for me!"*

And then he shared a priceless piece of wisdom: Generally, people not driven by money gain greater respect, and somehow money always finds them! And when it does, money doesn't change them!

"Handling classes meant hectic schedules and hardly any time with the family. So, why such a huge sacrifice if not for money?"

"Since my early days of teaching, I noticed that at least 10% of the students came from extremely poor families, and they struggled to pass CA because of their vernacular schooling backgrounds. They wouldn't even have the resources for three proper meals a day! And when they qualified CA, their entire family's standard of living improved! This ability to empower people and transform lives drove me!"

"Why then did you quit teaching, Sir?" I ask hesitantly.
"I believe in quitting at the peak!" he says, laughing.

MPV Sir may have stopped teaching, but he hasn't stopped inspiring! He continues to contribute to the CA fraternity through his speeches, technical sessions, and by his sheer presence!

Having written so much about him, I'd fail in my duty if I didn't tell you how to become an inspiration like him! He attributes his success to discipline and extreme hard work. *"I've always felt that I am not very intelligent, so I've always worked extremely hard to compensate for it!"*

Pointing to his protégé, he says, *"These guys were discussing a provision in GST today, and I had no clue about it! But I'll update in a day!"*

It was at this moment that I realised that MPV Sir's confidence and majesty come from his faith in his ability to work hard. He said that after turning 50, his hunger to learn and his appetite for hard work have only gone up! I had goosebumps! You should have been there to witness the majesty in his posture, the fire in his eyes, and the power in his voice when he said that! It was the roar of a lion proclaiming that even age cannot wane his might!

The pace of my heartbeat tells me that the interview has reached its peak, and since the accounting lion believes in quitting at the peak, I ask my final question: *"One piece of advice for aspiring CAs, Sir?"*

Without batting an eyelid, he said, *"Be convinced about the course and its ability to transform your life! Only if you believe that can you work hard and qualify! If you don't have that conviction, reach out to your mentors or elders who can give you that conviction. Have absolute faith in their words and work hard!"*

A tear rolled down my cheek because I know the story of a boy who had lost faith in this course and reached out to his mentor via an SMS. His mentor, who was an extremely busy man, found the time to call him and speak with him for an hour to convince the boy that qualifying CA could change his life! Thanks to the mentor's kindness and inspiration, the mentee worked hard and qualified CA—and his life truly changed!

The mentor: CA. M. P. Vijayakumar
The mentee: CA. P. Shandip Sabapathy

May we keep the tale of this Krishna alive—not just to glorify him, but so that countless Arjunas like you and me prosper!

FUELED BY FEAR

Ms. Swathi

AIR 30 – IPCC – Nov 2023

I am pleasantly surprised to learn that not all rank-holders are fueled by confidence or aspiration. Nearly half of the rank-holders I interviewed admitted that the fear of failure was the secret to their energy! Swathi confesses with utmost candor:

"Passing was the only choice! I've never faced failure. I really can't handle failure. So, I work incredibly hard to avoid it."

From Swathi, I learn that it is okay to be scared—as long as we use fear as fuel to perform better. As a student, I wasted countless precious hours paralyzed by fear. That's where the wise ones like Swathi stand out! She put in nine months of incredible effort—whether it was waking up at 3 a.m. or writing countless tests, she left no box unchecked in her pursuit of success.

"1. Planning well 2. Preparing & referring only to my handwritten notes, and 3. Chapter-wise cumulative revisions—these three strategies earned me a rank."

One common denominator in all my rank-holder interviews was that each one busted at least one myth I had about preparation, exams, or even life itself! I was blown away when Swathi said:

"Online classes played a huge role in my rank! I saved loads of time that would have been spent commuting, and I used all that saved time for my exam preparation."

I am amazed by how a tiny shift in perspective can cause a dramatic shift in experience. While most students lamented the disadvantages of online classes, Swathi chose to focus on the silver lining. Acceptance precedes adaptability. Swathi adapted to online classes swiftly and seamlessly—because she accepted the sudden change gracefully and interpreted it positively.

Such positivity can only spring from a grateful heart; Swathi is filled with gratitude towards her family, friends, and mentors—without whose steadfast support, this feat wouldn't have been possible.

I pause to allow these life lessons to sink in before asking, *"I'm clear about the mindset part now, but where do students go wrong in their preparation?"*

Swathi responds with absolute conviction:

"Lack of cumulative revision! They're satisfied with studying something just once. But repeated revisions alone help retain concepts until exams."

From my mentoring experience spanning a decade, I can vouch that Swathi is absolutely right!

For clarity's sake: Cumulative revision means revising all previous chapters before proceeding to a new one. While seemingly time-consuming, this method dramatically improves retention and saves a lot of time during the final stages of revision.

Like every other student, Swathi, too, had her fair share of low-performance days. She coped by sleeping and venting to loved ones. The trick is to find what works for you!

"But there's no point in pushing hard on your low days," says Swathi.

Noticing the time, I ask her one last question:

"Now that you've scored a rank in IPCC, is there added pressure for the Final?"

Swathi never jumps the gun; absorbing, reflecting, and then responding is her style. After a few moments of absolute silence, she replies:

"People around me expect more from me now, so there is definitely pressure. But it's up to me how I handle it! I have 2.5 years before my Final exams, but I've already begun my preparations."

Fear has already fueled her takeoff, and consistency shall ensure she reaches her destination.

Good luck, Swathi!

<u>Begin Early!</u>

Once upon a time, a snail was striving hard to climb a majestic tree. A tiny bird was amused by this sight and struck a conversation with the snail.

"Hey, why are you climbing this tree?" asked the bird.

Sweating and gasping, the snail slowly turned towards the bird and said, "What else would I climb this tree for? I'm climbing to eat the its fruits"

The bird rolled over laughing and said, "None of the fruits are ripe yet! They'll take days to ripen, so why are you climbing now!"

With the patience that comes only with wisdom, the snail replied, "Oh bird! When the fruits ripen you can just soar towards them and pluck them in an instant. But, considering my pace, I should begin crawling upward right now to be able to reach them when they're ripe!"

Takeaway:

Friends, the most common mistake among the student community is: starting late!

Only a handful can crack the exams or even score a rank with an effort spanning a few months; But most people would need months of untiring efforts to succeed!

And I'm absolutely confident, or even certain, that anyone can score a rank if they start early and work consistently!

TAKE CONTROL

CA. Chinmaya Hegde

AIR 13 – Foundation – May 2006
AIR 3 – Intermediate – Nov 2007
AIR 39 – Final – Nov 2010

Each of us is driven by our own core philosophies, and that philosophy serves as the compass that determines the direction and quality of our lives. CA Chinmaya's philosophy is simple:

"Don't go with the flow—take control!"

How else could the son of a petrol pump worker and a garment factory worker achieve an All India Rank in all three stages of an incredibly challenging course like Chartered Accountancy?

Every inch of Chinmaya's journey is awe-inspiring! Hailing from a family where his father worked at a petrol pump and his mother at a garment factory, Chinmaya studied in a Kannada-medium school until the 7th standard. In 8th, he transitioned to an English-medium school, which took a toll on his studies. I stared in disbelief when he said:

"I had absolutely no control over the subjects from 8th to 10th. I didn't want to continue that way, so I chose the commerce stream—new subjects would give me a fresh start! And that eventually led me to Chartered Accountancy."

Chinmaya didn't aim for a rank in the first two levels.

"My goal was simply to understand the concepts well so that I wouldn't have to study them again—considering the time crunch. I prepared charts for theory papers to condense the material."

However, when it came to the CA Final, he had 2.5 years to prepare—a good amount of time!

"I began classes two years before the exams (a masterstroke) and ticked off one subject at a time, alongside my articleship. I took three months per paper for classes plus self-study."

Beginning early and keeping it simple were the two most commonly used strategies among rank-holders.

Here are three practices Chinmaya swears by:

1. Concept clarity – Look for the logic. Ask yourself, "Why does this exist?" For practical papers, explore how to derive the formula.

2. Follow ICAI study material.

3. Prepare your own notes. If you're short on time, use highlighters to mark key points.

The greatest challenge in the CA preparation journey is handling the vast syllabus. Chinmaya recommends daily revision of what is taught in class that very day.

"Revise for 15 minutes that day and 15 minutes the next day. And never hesitate to ask questions in class."

In his opinion, the single biggest mistake most students make is focusing on results instead of efforts.

"When you want something, you've gotta become something. Become a knowledgeable, confident person with strong conceptual clarity, and the results will follow automatically."

In other words: Take control of the direction, and the destination will unfold automatically.

Chinmaya continues:

"Even if you don't score a rank, you have already become the person. You just haven't received the validation yet!"

I completely agree—the person you become is far more important than the validation you receive. Since Chinmaya speaks a lot about being and becoming, I am tempted to ask: What exactly is the mindset that creates rank-holders?

"What is a champion mindset?" I ask.

In his characteristic calm tone, he answers:

"Champions strategize. They know what they're good at, what they aren't good at, and they constantly play to their strengths!"

When I ask him for a piece of advice for readers, he instantly responds:

"Constantly work on improving yourself—you should be your first beneficiary! Apply the concepts you learn to your own life. If you can do this, a rank is a natural consequence."

Pro-tip: *Notice how Chinmaya's core philosophy—"Take control"—shapes every thought, response, and approach of his. Get your core philosophy right, and you will get your life right!*

Seven Valuable Insights from Chinmaya to Take Control of Your Exam Preparation:

1. Time is the key factor! Plan well—decide which subject or paper to begin with and the order in which you will proceed.

2. Start writing mock tests at least one month before the exams.

3. Ask yourself every day: "What is my most important duty today?" This will help you stay motivated and focused on your studies.

4. Don't compromise your studies for your office. Your studies will stay with you forever.

5. Don't avoid the challenges you face in your articleship. Those challenges help you grow.

6. Having a mentor is absolutely important! You should at least have someone to look up to.

7. There are two kinds of goals in life:

   - Effort goals – What you can directly control.
   - Result goals – What you can't directly control.
   - The more you focus on effort goals, the more your result goals will fall into place.

Lord Krishna, Swami Vivekananda, and CA Chinmaya Hegde all share the same gospel:

Don't go with the flow—**TAKE CONTROL!**

GOD OF SMALL THINGS

CA. C. N. Paramasivam

Inspiring CA

"A man is rich in proportion to the number of things he can afford to let alone!" – Henry David Thoreau.

If letting go is the measure of richness, then he is the richest Chartered Accountant I have ever come across!

He qualified as a Chartered Accountant and Company Secretary forty years ago, secured a position at a reputed company in Coimbatore, and had an exemplary stint there. And just as Prince Siddhartha (Gautama Buddha) quietly slipped out of his palace in search of truth, CA. C. N. Paramasivam walked away from the corporate palace in search of happiness, contentment, and peace.

Every chapter in this book has been written with the input and consent of the person featured in it—except this one! I didn't even inform him that he was being featured in my book because spotlights and fame make him squirm! He prefers anonymity and solitude.

His farm is his kingdom, solitude is his throne, contentment is his crown, his dogs are his generals, the birds are his messengers, and the trees are the subjects of his empire.

On days he wakes up late, his little winged friends anxiously scream from outside his window! Rain or shine, his typical day begins with feeding those tiny birds and watching them flutter away in contentment. The neighborhood children eagerly await his arrival, knowing he carries toffees for them every single day. Even at 70 years of age, he never forgets to call his teachers on every Teacher's Day.

He doesn't worry a bit when coconut prices hit rock bottom, but he grows extremely restless and anxious if anyone—be it pets or people— falls sick! To him, every life matters. Day in and day out, he tirelessly sows kindness and harvests happiness.

"You need to invest more time in the farm! Work harder!" he'd often insist.

Even at 70, he works so hard that every inch of his farm is ingrained in his muscle memory, and every tree speaks to him! And whenever people ask him why he has wasted his education, he looks at them intensely and says:

"You can never waste education! Education is a way of thinking. It has shaped who I am and drives the way I think and act."

Only after observing him closely did I realize that even the simplest of his farming decisions were derived from complex accounting tools, principles, and methods.

If you are someone who judges a book by its cover, you'd completely miss his greatness—because he carefully masks it with his characteristic simplicity.

Most people confuse contentment with laziness—but he taught me that they're two very different things!

He fondly reminds me often: *"Like Swami Vivekananda said, 'Consider yourself the trustee of your farm. Be detached, but work really hard.'"*

As my mentor, one of the first things he taught me was:

"If you spend enough time with trees, the trees will talk to you!"

He is so passionate about farming that even his metaphors, ideas, and philosophies are rooted in nature. And he is as much a teacher as he is a farmer!

Seeds of Wisdom He Sowed in Me:

1. Focus on the roots, and the fruits will follow.

2. Just as trees grow relentlessly in search of sunlight, keep growing relentlessly in search of wisdom.

3. Even the birds that migrate across continents find their way home without a GPS. That's proof that nature has given each one of us the intelligence we need to survive.

4. Even the best sapling cannot survive in the wrong soil. Choose your circle wisely.

5. People throw stones only at trees that bear fruit. If you're on a meaningful journey, be prepared for criticism.

6. Even the most fragrant flower will stink if you crush it and smell it. So, don't rub people the wrong way and then complain about their reaction!

7. As a tree grows taller, its roots must grow deeper. Otherwise, it will eventually fall—sooner or later. As you grow, remember to go deeper within yourself and stay rooted in self-awareness.

The sole purpose of featuring this enigma in a book about achievers is to tell you that accomplishments need not always be materialistic!

Pursuing wealth is intelligence. Pursuing what money can't buy is wisdom. If fame, money, and material accomplishments don't fascinate you, have the courage to throw them away and pursue your passion—or at least go in search of it!

CA. C. N. Paramasivam doesn't have a decorated profile to boast about—he doesn't even have a profile!

He isn't a child who doesn't understand the value of wealth and success.

He is a sage who chooses to live without them!

His happiness doesn't come from conquering—it comes from letting go.

And he finds glory not in grand achievements, but in the smallest of things, done with utmost passion, love, and kindness.

He is the god of small things. And he's my father too.

Go for the Sweets!

At the famous Kali temple in Dakshineswar, where the legendary Saint Sri Ramakrishna lived, his wife Sri Sarada Devi and a few disciples were on their toes making sweets for Navratri. Much to their annoyance, the minute they laid the plate of sweets on the floor, armies of ants swarmed towards them.

When all of their efforts to keep the ants at bay failed, Sri Ramakrishna said with a childlike laughter, "Why are you people struggling so much? Simply draw a circle around the tray of sweets using sugar! The ants would come and pick the sugar and head back without trying to approach the sweets!" And that's precisely what happened!

Sri Ramakrishna narrated this anecdote often to prod his disciples to pursue higher goals rather than settle for lesser pleasures as the ants did!

So, what are you going to do:

Settle for petty pleasures?

Or go past them towards the sweet tray that is a higher purpose?

THE EXTRA MILE

CA. Ishwarya Chandrasekaran

AIR 43 – IPCC – Nov 2016

"The difference between ordinary and extraordinary is that little extra!" –
Jimmy Johnson

Ishwarya's love for numbers led her to pursue CA, her faith in hard work pushed her to go the extra mile, and that extra mile rewarded her with an All India Rank!

She had to move to her grandmother's place for 11th grade because her hometown didn't have English-medium schools for higher secondary education. This should give you a glimpse of her humble beginnings.

I was curious—did she consciously aspire for greatness, or was greatness thrust upon her as a result of her hard work? Here's what she shared:

"Since I had put in a lot of effort in school, I didn't work really hard for my CA Foundation. Due to floods that affected many regions back

then, my exams got postponed by a fortnight. I ended up clearing my Foundation exams with just two weeks of preparation! That gave me the confidence that if I worked hard, I could score well. So, while attending IPCC classes, I made it a habit to study the day's topics on the same day. By the time my study holidays began, I had already completed three subjects! People around me started telling me I was ahead of the game, and that gave me the conviction that if I pushed harder, I could secure a rank."

Pro-tip: *I can never emphasize this enough—the single biggest decision that leads to securing a rank is starting early!*

Ishwarya had to juggle between college and IPCC classes. She had college from 7 a.m. to 12 p.m. and IPCC classes from 2 p.m. to 8 p.m. Yet, she managed to cover each day's topics that very day!

And during her study holidays, she maintained the same momentum, studying a minimum of 8 to 9 hours per day.

This is precisely what going the extra mile looks like!

"Wasn't it extremely challenging?" I ask, naively.

"No, sir. Since I was already used to sitting from 7 a.m. to 8 p.m. at my college and IPCC classes, it wasn't really challenging."

Pro-tip: *Like any other habit, the ability to study for long hours doesn't develop overnight. It must be built over time.*

This is where students who start preparing just a few months before exams lose out—because they don't give themselves enough time to build habits that will sustain them during the intensive preparation phase.

Every successful person I've featured in this book built their fortress of greatness on the foundation of daily habits.

Here are Ishwarya's three pillars of success:

1. Scheduling: I had a clear weekly schedule, and that helped me stay on track.

2. Consistency: I stuck to my study routine even on days I didn't feel like it.

3. Cutting out distractions: I avoided social media and anything else that could throw me off track.

"You make it sound so simple! Wasn't all this incredibly tough?" I press.

Without hesitation, she replies, *"Sir, I love to study. I enjoy it."*

This reminds me of a beautiful quote:

"The man who loves walking will walk further than the man who loves the destination."

The best way to increase your odds of success is to develop a passion for what you're pursuing.

One question I've asked almost every rank-holder is:

"What is an AIR mindset?"

Ishwarya's response is simple yet profound:

"You must have absolute clarity about your priorities and never deviate from them. At the student phase, nothing is more important than studies. This clarity + conviction = AIR mindset."

"What was your driving force to go the extra mile?" I ask.

Again, her reply is instant:

"My two elder sisters didn't have the privilege of pursuing professional education because they were married off at a young age. My parents gave me the opportunity to study, and I wanted to do justice to that!"

Ishwarya is a synonym for clarity—she doesn't mince words or second-guess herself!

She credits writing tests as the biggest contributor to her success.

"I wrote a lot of tests! Beyond the ones conducted by my academy, I wrote plenty of tests at home and self-evaluated them. I strongly recommend students evaluate their own tests instead of joining a test series. If you hand over that responsibility to an institution, you'll obsess over marks instead of learning where exactly you faltered."

To emphasize the importance of writing tests, Ishwarya adds:

"Sir, I wrote so many tests that when my academy conducted a test, I had already solved those very same questions before! I became so familiar with the exam that I knew exactly how I'd be tested, how much time I needed per question, and how fast I had to write. There wasn't a single exam I couldn't complete on time!"

Regardless of your age, gender, or background, the biggest challenge you'll face in your preparation journey is handling your own mind.

Many of Ishwarya's peers who began the IPCC journey with her had either decided to attempt only one group or chosen to skip the exam altogether. Yet, she remained unwavering in her conviction that she was on the right path.

Her teachers reassured her, and from that point onward—there was no looking back!

Since she had attended classes for all subjects, I asked her for tips to help students make the most of their classes. She shared two key pointers:

1. Have a study buddy to discuss what was taught in class. This helps ensure conceptual clarity.

2. By the end of each week, review and study everything covered that week. Simply watching lectures without complementing them with self-study is pointless!

She believes the biggest mistake students make today is not having clarity about their priorities and relying on shortcuts.

She strongly advises against shortcuts—because if you want to be extraordinary, you must be willing to go the extra mile!

When I ask her what securing a rank has given her, she lists two invaluable gifts:

1. *"Coming from a village, I always felt I was lagging behind my batchmates in Coimbatore. They had far more exposure than me, and I was intimidated. But after securing a rank, they all started recognizing me—and that boosted my confidence."*

2. *"A rank opens doors. I have an edge over those who don't have one."*

One final piece of advice for students?

"Strive to pass on your first attempt! It's so much easier than preparing for multiple attempts."

Just as a compass always points north, Ishwarya always points toward going the extra mile!

If you want to meet Ishwarya, be willing to go the extra mile!

That's where you'll find her—always.

HUSTLE AND GRIND

CA. Sri Ram

AIR 7 – IPCC – May 2013
AIR 1 – Final – May 2016

"Success is no accident. It is hard work, perseverance, learning, studying, sacrifice, and, most of all, love for what you are doing or learning to do!" said the legendary footballer Pelé. Sri Ram quite literally lived this quote to earn his All India Rank 1 in the CA Final!

Born and brought up in Salem, Sri Ram was the typical small-town schoolboy who thrived in the comfort of his cocoon. It's no wonder, then, that he chose CA—just so he wouldn't have to leave town for college!

"I was introduced to Chartered Accountancy in my 7th grade, thanks to a few CAs in my extended family. The biggest incentive for choosing CA was that I could skip going to college. That meant I didn't have to stress over 10th and 12th standard public exams—those grades don't matter if you're

not applying to college. Another major plus was that this qualification would allow me to either seek employment or start my own firm."

Once he had made his choice in 7th grade, his interest in science subjects waned, and his marks in those subjects dipped. This meant no credentials like State Topper, District Topper, or even School Topper!

"But that was a conscious choice. 'If you decide to do CA, then forget about 11th and 12th—let's prepare for CA Foundation,' my mom said. She got me the Foundation books, and I began preparing in 11th standard. I also took additional classes in Hindi, Sanskrit, typewriting, and shorthand because my mom believed that continuous engagement with various subjects would help me develop the habit of working hard while also honing my ability to manage multiple courses at the same time—both of which would come in handy for CA. Besides, I'd need these skills as a Chartered Accountant! These classes kept me on my toes, and studying for 7-8 hours a day became a habit. As a result, I scored 180 out of 200 in my CPT (CA Foundation) exams."

A natural consequence of scoring high is the visibility, attention, and valuable guidance that follow. Who doesn't like to bet on a winning horse? Some wise Chartered Accountants encouraged Sri Ram to aim for an All India Rank, marking the beginning of his journey to greatness.

"Consistent hard work paid off—I secured AIR 7 in the IPCC exams. I could have joined any audit firm of my choice, but I decided against doing my articleship at a Big 4 firm. My father was just recovering from tuberculosis, and my mother was already living three hours away because of her work. Also, we couldn't afford a big enough space in Chennai for my father and me, since our family was surviving solely on my mother's income."

I am truly amazed to learn that Sri Ram's father opted for early retirement solely to support his son's ambitions! *"My parents were absolutely clear that one of them would stay home to support me in every possible way."*

Pro-tip: *The support of your family is absolutely crucial in any ambitious endeavor. Have an open conversation with them about the importance of a rank and the support you need.*

If scoring 180 in CPT gave him visibility, his AIR 7 in IPCC magnified it manifold! Sri Ram now had plenty of opportunities to address fellow students. *"At my first public speaking opportunity, I couldn't speak for more than two minutes! Meanwhile, my friends—who were great orators—spoke about me for 15 minutes. My mentor advised me to join the CA student body, SICASA, to develop my communication and leadership skills.*

I became an active member, and during my tenure as secretary, we organized over 100 events in a year. That year, the Salem SICASA won its first-ever Best Branch award at the national level! Along the way, I delivered countless speeches and presented 4-5 papers at state and national-level student conferences. All of this helped me hone my communication and leadership skills."

Pro-tip: *The three pillars of success in this profession are:*

1. *Academics*

2. *Practical knowledge gained through articleship*

3. *Communication, leadership, and allied skills*

Most students make the mistake of focusing excessively on one pillar while neglecting the other two.

Sri Ram, however, was different! He wasn't a bookworm who confined himself to his studies—he was a social butterfly who pursued his passions. *"I loved spending time with friends, playing badminton, and watching movies—I didn't want to miss out on any of these! My father and I would agree on a weekly study target, and as long as I met that goal, I was free to do whatever I wanted. My father would jot down my daily study hours on a calendar and keep me informed about my progress."*

Sri Ram says it was this planning and consistency that helped him secure a rank. But it didn't just earn him one rank—it earned him four! He secured:

- AIR 7 in IPCC
- AIR 1 in CS Intermediate
- AIR 1 in CA Final (the cherry on top!)
- AIR 6 in CS Final

Sri Ram is living proof that hard work always pays off!

Since many of the rank-holders I interviewed claimed that fear pushed them toward greatness, I asked Sri Ram if he felt the same. His response was insightful:

"Fear is something you can't completely eliminate. I'd be surprised if champions like Sachin Tendulkar or Virat Kohli weren't afraid of getting out while batting! It's normal to be frightened—but letting fear demotivate you is the real problem."

Sri Ram had mentioned in a YouTube interview that he still makes time on weekends to guide aspiring CA students. When I asked what drives him to do that, he reflected for a moment before saying,

"When I decided to pursue CA, the noise around me was all negative: 'CA is extremely tough,' 'Not everyone can crack it,' 'You should have a Plan B,' and so on. After qualifying, I realized that most of those statements were wrong! I've always wished I had more positive mentors back then.

I see so many Sri Rams out there—students who want to succeed but lack proper guidance. I sincerely hope that my 30-45 minutes of conversation with them plays at least a small role in helping them achieve their goals. That being said, I hardly get 4-5 calls a year!"

I ask Sri Ram if all AIR rank-holders are geniuses, and he responds instantly,

"Yes, they are! But no one is born a genius—you become one by following the 3 Ps: Planning, Preparation, and Practice. If someone is consistent in these three areas, they will undoubtedly achieve greatness in their field."

Consistency is a challenge even for champions, but Sri Ram had a secret weapon—his father. His dad tracked his study hours meticulously. *"The deal was that I had to study 15 hours a week, alongside articleship and classes. Once I hit that target, I could do whatever I wanted. Every Saturday, my dad would do the math and let me know how many more hours I needed to study to reach my goal."*

To combat negativity, Sri Ram took an unusual approach:

"In October 2015, my dad wrote on a big chart: 'CA. Sri Ram, AIR 1 – May 2016 Final Exam.' All my friends saw it. This was my way of proving my commitment—while they worried about just clearing the exam, I had my eyes on a bigger goal. It seemed small at the time, but in hindsight, I realize it played a crucial role in my AIR 1."

Sri Ram attributes his success to three daily habits:

1. Consistent preparation—clocking two hours of study daily, no matter what.

2. Enjoying life—his time with SICASA helped him maintain balance.

3. Taking breaks—he spent Sundays from 3 p.m. to 9 p.m. with friends.

When asked what his rank has given him, he says, *"The benefits are mostly lifestyle-related. I can afford to be generous with my time and money, but only because my rank gave me this lifestyle. It also helped me build a strong network across India."*

"There are no shortcuts to any place worth going." —Beverly Sills

So, if you want to attain greatness, be prepared to hustle and grind!

<u>The Power of Habit</u>

In his very inspiring and innovative book 'The power of habit', Charles Duhigg outlines a strategy to build or break habit chains!

Charles Duhigg says that every habit has 3 elements:

1. Cue: The trigger that initiates the habit, like seeing a certain food or feeling stressed.

2. Routine: The actual tasks performed, like eating the food or drinking out of stress.

3. Reward: The happiness, satisfaction, or relief you feel after performing the routine. This reward becomes the cue for the next routine, thus forming a habit-loop!

To build a habit, make the cue easily accessible:

To increase your probability of eating fruits, you have to place them where you see them everyday. I.e. on your dining table, not in the tray at the bottom of your fridge!

I always nudge my mentees to have a written study schedule as it would keep reminding them how far they've come and how far they ought to go. And knowing the amount of portions pending is a strong cue that triggers the routine of studies! From personal experience: when you study consistently for a few days, and tick those portions in your written schedule: you'd notice your self-esteem rising higher and that reward (dopamine or feeling good) will induce you to keep going!

One game-changer for me was: glancing at my next day's schedule and planning the next day – each night before hitting bed. I've noticed that when our mind has absolute clarity about what to do, it happily cooperates with us; but when it doesn't have clarity about what to do it will resist in a thousand ways, and we'd end up not doing the task!

To break a habit, make the cue difficult to access or replace the bad cue with a good cue:

The best way to avoid eating junk is not having them at home!

Your smartphone can easily become the greatest obstacle or impediment on your path to success! Never carry your mobile to your study room!

I wear a watch not just to see time, but also to save time! I observed that whenever I used my phone to check time, I'd end up responding to the notifications displayed, thereby losing the precious time I wanted to track! Using a wristwatch saves me from that trouble!

From the food industry to the technology sector, most huge corporates have a team of psychologists or behaviourists working towards keeping its customers hooked to their products! So please be absolutely aware about what habits you're building; one addiction is enough to drag you down!

Use this piece of knowledge to build habits that help you build the future you desire!

RISE IN LOVE!

CA. S. D. Balasubramanyan

Inspiring CA

A young lad once fell in love but couldn't pursue it, owing to his family circumstances. Almost four decades later, he decided to search for his lost love! After countless struggles, he finally found it—and they lived happily ever after! Sounds like the script of a Bollywood movie, doesn't it?

Well, this is the life story of a marvellous man named CA. S. D. Balasubramanyan and his never-ending love for the vocation called Chartered Accountancy.

S. D. Bala Sir, as he is fondly called by his students across the globe, fell in love with the Chartered Accountancy profession in his teens, thanks to the many CAs in his extended family. However, due to family circumstances, he had to take the bank exams and join the State Bank of India as a probationary officer. His dexterity and work ethic helped him rise to the position of Deputy General Manager.

After a 20-year stint at SBI, he took early retirement and joined Sundaram Finance.

Though he had a successful career, his love for Chartered Accountancy still lingered. And at the age of 56, he decided to quit his job and pursue CA!

He makes it all sound so easy:

"I asked my wife if we could manage with my existing savings and pension, and she said yes. So, I quit my job and plunged into CA! I passed CA Intermediate with self-study. For CA Final, I rented a flat, got myself a scooter, and relocated to Chennai with my mother and wife."

"Sir, you make it sound so easy, but what was it really like, attending classes with kids three decades younger than you?" I ask curiously.

With the classic S. D. Bala smile, he replies:

"I don't know if they were encouraged, but I certainly was! The faculty were all supportive, and my wife and mother stood by me every step of the way. My needs were always met, regardless of how much money we had."

Just as I am about to shoot my next question, the cook walks in, and Bala Sir asks her to serve us tea:

"They've come to write nice things about me, so give them good tea; please don't give them the tea you give me every day!"

If Chartered Accountancy was his love, humor was his best buddy! Watching him crack jokes is a treat—the twinkle in his eye and a naughty smile are preludes to every joke of his. When that twinkle and smile appear, you'd better be ready to laugh your heart out!

I resume the interview: *"What was the greatest challenge you faced as a student?"*

"Writing speed was my biggest challenge! I didn't have to write much at work, and my writing skills had naturally waned. But as a CA student, I had to write around 30 pages in three hours."

Now comes the twinkle, the smile, and the poster-worthy quote:

"Usain Bolt can't sit with his eyes closed and say, 'I'm running, I'm running really fast, I've finished first!' He has to do real field practice."

And then, with a piercing look, he asks:

"How different is having to write 30 pages in three hours?"

He was determined to train himself every day.

"I'd literally copy my book. I did it so regularly that eventually, I could write 40 pages in three hours! And there wasn't a single paper I couldn't finish on time!"

He chuckles as he recalls how his son would check on him daily, ensuring he met his writing goals. Bala Sir even sought out a registered exam paper valuer to learn how to present his paper better!

Just imagine having the passion and determination to do all this at 58 years of age!

When Keanu Reeves was once asked, *"Are you a lover or a fighter?"* he said:

"If you're a lover, you gotta be a fighter. If you don't fight for your love, what kind of love do you have?"

S. D. Bala Sir was as much a fighter as he was a lover!

Noticing that I am lost in awe, he gently brings me back to the interview.

"Despite all these efforts, I failed my first attempt. It was in my second attempt that I qualified as a CA. Please mention that in the book—I want people to know!"

Ponder on this for a moment: the co-author of your CA textbooks wants the world to know that he too failed in his CA exams!

How's that for humility?

This is a true aha moment for me—or rather, for the psychologist in me! It is at this moment that I realize that his constant happiness comes from never taking himself too seriously. His greatness is soaked in humility.

After qualifying as a Chartered Accountant, he practiced for a while, but he was more of a teacher and author than a conventional practitioner. He co-authored over a dozen books, all of which he had on his bookshelf.

With the enthusiasm of a child showing off his toys, he proudly explains his books to us! They are his trophies, his milestones, and above all, his contribution to the fraternity he loved so much.

When CA students requested him to handle Accounting Standards classes at the Coimbatore Branch of ICAI, he happily obliged. When they said there wouldn't be more than 20 students, he said:

"Even if one person is willing to learn, I'm willing to teach."

And he taught without charging a single rupee—that was his love for the CA fraternity and its student community!

"Why so much love for Chartered Accountancy? What has CA really given you?" I ask curiously.

A minute of silence prevails, and my heart is in my throat, wondering if I have offended him.

With a disarming smile, he says:

"It has given me so much worldly exposure and has made me a confident person. Thanks to the CA qualification, I came across many learned people like CA. T. N. Manoharan, CA. M. P. Vijay Kumar, CA. Pattabhi Ram, and CA. P. Shandip Sabapathy."

When he utters my name, my heart almost pops out!

That is S. D. Bala for you. In his loving eyes, everyone is special and worth being celebrated!

His qualification, contributions, and credentials are only his accomplishments. But his legacy is so much more than that—it was the person he was!

Yes, the person he was.

Just as I was about to mail this write-up for his approval, I got the shocking news of his demise. When we went to pay our last respects, I told his family about the interview.

His son said, *"Consider it approved."*

And his wife, with that same childlike smile of her husband, said:

"But you need my approval too!"

I was amazed to learn that humility, kindness, and greatness weren't just Bala Sir's virtues—they ran in his entire family.

With a heavy heart, I glanced at the mortal remains of this great man—there he lay, with a calm and contented expression. Even death could not steal his grace!

There was a tiny smile on his face, and I was reminded of the lyrics from a Rajinikanth movie:

"Happiness is the prerogative of children and the enlightened ones."

I know not if Bala Sir was a child or a sage—or a bit of both. But I know this for sure:

He was an **epitome of love!**

Love you, Bala Sir!

ONE DAY AT A TIME

CA. Hamsa Narasimhan

AIR 29 – CA Foundation – Nov 2019

Six hours of college and six hours of CA Foundation classes were his daily routine. Hamsa Narasimhan had to somehow find time for self-study amidst this hectic schedule. And he did—well enough to score above 80% and secure an All India Rank in his CA Foundation exams!

While mediocre people find excuses for not performing, extraordinary people find reasons to excel. When I ask him what kept him going, he says with a chuckle, *"Lack of time! That was a blessing in disguise, sir. I had no time to think."*

I always tell my mentees that one sign of effective preparation is absolute certainty about passing when you walk out of an exam hall. While Hamsa Narasimhan was confident about passing, little did he expect an All India Rank.

"Despite cracking the AIR code in Foundation, why didn't you score a rank in IPCC and Final?" I ask. With utmost candor, he replies, *"Sir, while CA Foundation is a 100-meter sprint, IPCC and Final are marathons! I am a sprinter, not a marathoner."* His clarity about his strengths and weaknesses is impressive!

But such clarity and wisdom don't come easily. Hamsa, too, learned things the hard way. Like most students, he lost many days to overthinking and anxiety.

"No matter what, everyone is sailing in the same boat. We should remind ourselves of this and stay calm. In my opinion, calmness is as important as exam preparation. Another costly mistake was taking my physical and mental health for granted; my body and mind gave up, and I couldn't recall even the portions I knew so well!"

"So, how can sprinters like you score a rank in the IPCC and Final marathons?" I ask. After mulling over the question for a few minutes, he says that it isn't necessary to study 12-15 hours a day! His advice is to be consistent with whatever hours you can clock and to do one or two things you enjoy daily to stay relaxed.

When I ask him what, according to him, defines an AIR mindset, he says, *"Don't have a Plan B!"* Then, he adds something absolutely profound: *"If you set a small target, you'll definitely fall short. Look at CA as just one lap in the race called life. Life is so much bigger, and we ought to learn to see the bigger picture!"*

And Hamsa Narasimhan lives by his philosophy that giving your 100% is the only way to avoid regrets. *"If you give your 100%, you won't be affected by the results—even if you fail!"* he assures.

Since he emphasizes the bigger picture, I ask him what skills would help people master it, and he names public speaking, technological prowess, and reading as the three most essential skills.

I ask him my last question with a bit of hesitation, *"Life is a marathon, but you are a sprinter! How are you even managing?"*

And with a classic Hamsa Narasimhan smile, he offers another profound piece of wisdom: *"Sir, I can manage one day at a time. So, like Dale Carnegie recommends, I think one day at a time, and I give my 100% every single day."*

For a moment, I felt like the student Shifu, learning from his teacher, Master Oogway, in the marvelous movie *Kung Fu Panda*. Master Oogway, too, often reminded those around him, *"Yesterday is history, tomorrow is a mystery, but today is a gift. That is why it is called the present."*

Whether you see life as a race, a marathon, or a journey, one thing is certain—living one day at a time is the recipe for happiness and peace.

Thank you, Hamsa Narasimhan, for this wisdom!

<u>Google Map</u>

I read a beautiful note that said:

When you take a wrong turn, the google map doesn't scold, mock, or even blame. It simply guides you to the right path. Be like google map!

If you've taken a wrong route,

If you've gone a long way in that route,

If you've lost a lot of time because of this,

It's okay. Please don't be harsh on yourself!

Like the Google map, gently navigate yourself to the right path.

This will help you avoid road closures,

And that is the fastest route to success and happiness!

Happy travelling!

NOT ALL THOSE WHO WANDER ARE LOST!

CA. Lakshmanan Arasu

AIR 2 – IPCC – May 2018

In a world filled with travelers pursuing milestones, rare are those who wander aimlessly on the shores of knowledge! They fight not for fame or golden thrones but for the sheer joy of fighting. They play not for trophies or rewards but for the sheer joy of playing. They learn not for recognition or hefty paychecks but for the sheer joy of learning.

As I wandered aimlessly on the shores of compassion, a fellow wanderer waved at me from the shores of knowledge, and we began wandering together thereafter—as mentor and mentee!

So here's how the story began:

Lakshman was working for Infosys and was unhappy with corporate life. But he lacked clarity about what he truly wanted. That's when his father recommended Chartered Accountancy. When Lakshman asked what CA was all about, his father simply said, "2+3 = 5. *That's what CA is about.*" And just like that, Lakshman took the plunge, leaving behind a lucrative job!

"Weren't you scared?" I ask.

After flashing his characteristic Colgate smile, Lakshman replies, *"A lot of people warned me that CA is tough—especially for someone with an engineering background. But the ones who knew me well said, 'Yes, it's tough, but you can definitely do it!'"*

That's when we met—at the 15-day Orientation Programme conducted by the Coimbatore Branch of the Institute of Chartered Accountants of India. At that time, he had just begun studying 11th standard accountancy! From there, he soared to an All India Rank 2 in his IPCC exams!

Here are some aspects he got right to achieve his rank:

1. Adequate time – *"I got my SRO late, which gave me around 1.5 years to prepare. That extra time allowed me to go from the basics of accountancy to mastering IPCC subjects."*

2. Reaching out for help – *"I left a gap of three months between classes and self-study, which was a huge blunder. I completely forgot what had been taught, and I was shattered. Thankfully, I reached out to my sister Vishalakshi (who was also pursuing CA), and she reassured me that everything I had learned was still within me—I just had to retrieve it. My mother was also a pillar of strength during my emotional lows."*

3. Joining the mentoring program – *"It was during our mentoring process that you planted the idea of an All India Rank! I remember you suddenly declaring, 'Lakshman, we are getting a rank!' And I exclaimed, 'Sir, you're saying it so casually—like we're about to buy a kilo of potatoes!'"*

4. Consistency in practices – *"I was 100% consistent with visualization and water anchoring, as you recommended—even on days when I was feeling low."*

Lakshman's preparation timeline looked like this:

- 7 months of classes – He built a solid foundation by being 100% attentive and consistent.

- 3-month break – A major blunder.

- 4 months of full-time study – He accelerated, closed the gap, and raced past the finish line!

"During the seven months of classes, I never skipped a single session for any reason. I was 100% attentive and never hesitated to ask doubts."

"And in the four months of full-time study, I got these elements right:"

1. A well-planned, written schedule.

2. Consistency in daily routines.

3. Regular revisions.

4. Reaching out for help when needed.

5. 20-minute power naps at noon to keep the second half productive.

6. Frequent tests to realistically assess my preparation and boost confidence.

"What were the specific challenges of transitioning from engineering to accountancy?" I ask.

A brief silence follows—he seems to be revisiting those days.

**"The challenges were twofold: external and internal.*

The external challenge was the judgments and gossip about my leap from Infosys to CA. My family shielded me from much of it.

The internal challenge was the self-doubt—whether this truly fascinated me. I told myself that once I gained conceptual clarity, interest would naturally follow. So I kept reading books, interacting with people, and browsing Investopedia to strengthen my understanding.

Sir, I'd like to reiterate: unless we ask, people can't help. Whenever we're stuck, we should ask for help without worrying about our image. Ask, and it shall be given! People expect clarity to come to them—it won't! We have to seek it."

Even our mentoring journey began because of his constant searching and asking. One day, he ran up to me, shared his background, and asked if I could mentor him for his exams!

"For the benefit of readers, how did mentoring help you?" I prod.

Lakshman sums it up in three points:

1. It was a catalyst – *"I learned effective preparation methods, which saved me a lot of time and effort."*

2. A safe space – *"You provided a non-judgmental space where I could vent my frustrations."*

3. Accountability – *"Staying accountable kept me on track. If we can't honor self-boundaries, we need external accountability."*

One of Lakshman's strongest qualities is his brutal honesty. The moment I tell him I'm interviewing him for this book, he says, *"Sir, please write about my mistakes too—the students should know!"* He never minces words or sugarcoats opinions. So I ask, *"What are the three biggest mistakes students make?"*

Without hesitation, he replies:

1. Not having a strong purpose.

2. Lack of faith or self-belief.

3. Avoiding self-evaluation through tests. – *"Most students evade tests because they don't want their fantasies shattered."*

"Since purpose was your first point, what was your purpose?" I ask curiously.

"I didn't want to be the wrong example, sir! I didn't want people to say, 'If you wander from your path like Lakshman, you'll get lost and perish.' I wanted to prove that not all those who wander are lost!"

By now, if you're wondering how Lakshman, with all this wisdom, missed a rank in CA Final, here's how:

1. He repeated the same mistake of taking a break between classes and self-study. *"Readers, never repeat your mistakes—you'll regret it!"*
2. COVID struck like a tsunami – Social media was flooded with rumors about exam postponements, and he got lost in that noise.

In my opinion, letting go of the mentoring process was another mistake. *"Never change what's working, as long as it is working."* After his IPCC rank, I offered to mentor him for his Final exams for free. But Lakshman wanted to test himself, despite my caution against taking such a huge risk at a critical juncture. Mentoring would have certainly helped him avoid the two costly mistakes he mentioned.

A gentle disclaimer: Any reference to mentoring here is to emphasize the importance of a support system—not necessarily my mentoring.

But Lakshman is someone who sees even weeds as flowers. He's happy he failed, for it taught him that the process is what truly matters!

Anyway, all's well that ends well! Lakshman qualified as a CA on his second attempt. Brushing aside countless lucrative offers, he partnered with his good friend, CA. Maalan Barathi (yet another wanderer), and established a firm of his own. Alongside his Chartered Accountancy practice, Lakshman also pursues his passion for speaking and teaching. Not all those who wander are lost!

As I finish writing this chapter, my clock screams at me—it's high time I wind up and hit the sack. But first, I must write in my gratitude journal:

I am grateful for having mentored the finest mentee the world has ever seen!

DON'T EVER GIVE UP!

CA. T. Suganthi

Inspiring CA

I squirm with shame when CA. T. Suganthi proclaims that she had 100% attendance in her CA Intermediate classes! Is that even an accomplishment worth raving about?

Well, the classes took place on the second floor of a building that didn't have an elevator! In case you're wondering, how does that make it an accomplishment?

Suganthi can't walk! She had to literally crawl her way up to the second floor to attend classes, and yet, she didn't miss a single class!

"If you can't fly, then run. If you can't run, then walk. If you can't walk, then crawl. But whatever you do, you have to keep moving!"

Martin Luther King Jr. said these words, and Suganthi literally crawled her way to greatness!

Life is not the same for differently-abled people as it is for you and me. They have to design their lives around their disabilities, and they must fight even for the basic privileges we take for granted.

Suganthi was affected by polio when she was just 1.5 years old, and she chose commerce solely because her physical condition made it impossible for her to stand and work in a laboratory.

"I had applied for B.Com at Lady Doak College in my hometown, Madurai. People with lower scores than mine got admission letters, but I didn't. The reason? The principal of the college believed that disabled students would quit midway for various reasons. Her apprehensions were valid in a way—we had to shuttle between different blocks for various classes, which was extremely challenging for disabled students."

After a lot of convincing, the principal granted her admission—on the condition that Suganthi's parents buy her a wheelchair.

On the first day of college, all the students were surprised to see that the commerce block now had a new ramp. Courtesy: our Wonder Woman!

Just like any other college, the students were busy frolicking, while Suganthi was busy waging the war of life. Once you set your eyes on greatness, you just can't rest till you get there.

Thanks to the advice of a Chartered Accountant, she decided to pursue Chartered Accountancy and joined Foundation classes.

"My college would end at 3 p.m., and from there, I'd somehow reach my classes by 3:30 p.m. It was incredibly challenging, but the hard work paid off, and I was one of just six people who succeeded in the May 2000 examination out of 306 candidates!

I had to drop out of college, just as my principal had feared, and I sat there with bated breath, clueless about how she'd respond. But she was genuinely thrilled that I was pursuing a mightier goal!"

She moved from Madurai to Coimbatore to pursue Chartered Accountancy, and then came the challenge of finding a suitable CA firm for her articleship. The only criterion was that the office had to be on the ground floor—fortunately, she found and joined a suitable one.

Then came the challenge of commuting to different places for classes.

Suganthi's mother got her a Kinetic Honda and modified it to suit her needs. Suganthi learned to drive it in a single day!

One common thread among physically challenged people is that even everyday life is a battle—and just like any other battle, it requires the collective effort of an entire battalion!

Her father, a government employee at the TWAD Board, got himself transferred to Coimbatore to support his daughter. Her mother, a staff member at BSNL, had to live miles away due to work commitments.

Her brother supported Suganthi to the best of his abilities.

Even Suganthi's interview was a team effort! Her loving father and extremely supportive husband were by her side, filling in the blanks and nudging her to share specific anecdotes.

"Please share about your CA student journey," I request.

"I was blessed with a good study group, which gave me the right environment to work hard. I cleared my Intermediate exams on the very first attempt in November 2001. But then, my entire study group moved to Chennai for CA Final classes, and I was left behind. I longed to go, but it was impossible for my father to get another transfer to accompany me."

I am curious to know how she fared in her CA Final exams.

"I wrote both groups and failed twice. Naturally, people advised me to take one group at a time. But I persisted! My father took me to CA Badrinarayanan Sir for counseling. He helped me realize that my fears and insecurities were holding me back."

Suganthi had a massive insecurity—she believed that not attending classes in Chennai would sabotage her performance.

That fear was dragging her down.

Thanks to Badrinarayanan Sir's guidance, she shed those insecurities and sought alternative ways to compensate. She attended crash courses at ICAI's Tirupur branch.

"To attend those crash courses, we had to take the train every weekend. My father carried me on his shoulder between platforms just to get me there on time! We often stayed at relatives' or friends' houses. But we made it work. And it paid off—I qualified as a Chartered Accountant in May 2004."

Her father interjects, *"Every step of this journey was a battle, an experience, and an anecdote worth sharing! Our story can't be captured in just a few hours or confined to a few pages."*

That was no exaggeration. Every step was filled with unforeseen challenges, extraordinary effort, and surprising victories.

Suganthi attended the campus placement at ICAI, Chennai. Thanks to CA T. N. Manoharan, a council member at the time, she was exempted from the cap on the number of interviews a candidate could attend.

She aced interviews at six companies, including Satyam, Saint-Gobain, and Dhanlaxmi Bank.

And if you ever meet CA Suganthi in person, this wouldn't surprise you—her passion and optimism are contagious!

On TNM Sir's advice, she chose Dhanlaxmi Bank. Two years later, she moved to ICICI as an Assistant Manager – Credit (Rural Banking).

During her tenure at ICICI, she conducted a site visit to a tea factory in the Nilgiris and wrote a detailed report. It was so exhaustive that the national head of ICICI's credit division turned it into the company's official SOP (Standard Operating Procedure), circulating it nationwide!

And this is just one of countless testaments to her passion, knowledge, and skill.

In 2010, she joined BSNL as a Junior Accounts Officer, where she has worked ever since.

Imagine a Paralympic athlete being pushed to compete at the Olympics—that's how life is for the differently-abled!

Qualifying as a Chartered Accountant is an achievement in itself. Accomplishing this despite overwhelming challenges? That's legendary!

What makes Suganthi truly special is that she has never allowed life's trials to rob her of her confidence, her smile, or her warmth.

I ask, *"Didn't you ever feel disadvantaged? Weren't you tempted to play the victim card?"*

She responds instantly, *"Disability didn't strike me suddenly. I've only ever known myself this way. So I've never felt incomplete or disadvantaged. In 5th standard, after surgery, I had to choose between treatment and education. I chose education—and I'm glad I did! Besides CA, I also hold a B.Com, CAIIB, and an MBA in Banking & Finance. I am the breadwinner of my family and contribute meaningfully to society. Life is beautiful—I have no regrets!"*

I ask how CA has impacted her life. She pauses, eyes closed, as silence fills the room.

Finally, she says, *"I realized the magic of the words 'Chartered Accountant' only after qualifying. It evokes trust and respect. Now, people don't see me as a disabled woman. They see me as a Chartered Accountant. And that gives me immense confidence! I can now guide and empower many others—especially disabled women."*

CA T. Suganthi has inspired countless lives and won numerous awards. But for her, accolades are just byproducts. Her true purpose? To inspire others.

"If I could achieve so much despite my disability, so can others! My life is my message."

Any advice for my readers Ma'am?

"Sure! **Failure isn't a sin—it's just a setback. Don't ever give up!"**

This isn't just advice.

It's her mantra. Her motto. Her life.

How Badly?

Legend has it that a young man once asked Socrates the secret to success. Socrates told the young man to meet him near the river the next morning. They met and Socrates asked the young man to walk with him to the river. When they were neck-deep in water, Socrates pushed the Man under the water. The young lad struggled to get out but Socrates kept him there, until he turned blue. Finally, when Socrates raised the lad's head out of the water, the first thing he did was to take a deep breath of air.

Socrates asked, "What did you want the most when you were under water?" The boy replied, "Air."

Socrates said with a smile, "When you want success as badly as you wanted air, you will have it. That is the secret to success."

FLOAT LIKE A BUTTERFLY, STING LIKE A BEE!

CA. Natarajan AR

AIR 15 – Foundation – Nov 2019
AIR 14 – IPCC – Nov 2020
AIR 13 – Final – Nov 2023

Flabbergasted (adjective)
Meaning: extremely surprised or astonished.

I've come across this word countless times, and I've even used it innumerable times, but for the first time ever, I experienced it—thanks to Natarajan!

With three months left before exams—when most people subscribe to test series—Natarajan subscribed to Netflix and Hotstar! *"Watching Cook with Comali and F.R.I.E.N.D.S helped me de-stress. So I watched them for one hour each day. That's also when I am active on social media—when you're racing hard, that's when you need the pit stop the most."*

I am literally flabbergasted! *"What? But didn't that affect the quality of your studies?"* I ask anxiously, and his calm response is: *"When you have a strong purpose, nothing can distract or disturb you. I was absolutely clear that the only purpose of the breaks was to help me work harder—just as a Formula One racer hits the pit stop only to go faster!"* Natarajan's approach reminded me of Muhammad Ali's famous quote: *"Float like a butterfly, sting like a bee!"*

But that doesn't mean you can compromise on the basics! Natarajan (and Muhammad Ali) never compromised on fundamentals—like getting eight hours of quality sleep, maintaining a healthy diet, and taking enough breaks to prevent burnout.

Planning in advance helped him stay on track without having to push too hard. While pushing too hard can give you an adrenaline rush and even make you feel heroic, it will wear you down soon. The CA preparation journey is a marathon, not a sprint.

Natarajan had three layers (or levels) of planning:

1. A macro plan for the five months of revision.
2. A micro plan for the current month.
3. A sub-plan for the next day.

"Well-planned is half done! External circumstances can always throw you off your plan. That's where family support becomes crucial!" he reminds me.

Pro-tip: *Before you begin your preparation journey, talk to your family about your purpose, its importance, and the support you expect from them. This makes it easier for them to support you—and for you to focus on your journey.*

Most students have the misconception that three is the golden number when it comes to revisions; Natarajan strongly advises against this.

"There were subjects for which I did only two revisions, and there were subjects for which I had six revisions! There's no golden number; the number of revisions should be decided solely by how well you grasp a subject."

But the above is possible only when you begin early! According to Natarajan, the biggest—and most common—mistake is starting late. "Out of the ten peers in my office, I was the only one to begin classes two years be*fore my exams!"*

At the risk of sounding stupid, I ask, *"So what exactly were the advantages of starting early?"*

Starting early gave me three advantages:

- I could create notes on A4 sheets—confine each chapter to a single sheet—and that was a game changer! It helped me revise effectively in the one-and-a-half days between exams.

- I could revise every single portion within five days of my initial study.

- I could complete the classes during my articleship period, which gave me five whole months for revision and for working through plenty of past exam question papers.

Pro-tip: *Plan to complete your classes and initial study during your two years of articleship so that you can use the eight-month waiting period for your SPOMs, AICTSS, and revisions.*

If you're wondering whether a rank is worth all these efforts, Natarajan says, "A one-time effort will yield fruits for a lifetime! A rank doubles your opportunities; many mighty corporates open their doors only for rank holders."

He then says something absolutely simple yet profound: *"If you are a rank-holder, you are on the demand side of the equation; otherwise, you end up falling on the supply side of the equation, and that obviously diminishes your value!"* Once again, I am flabbergasted!

Regardless of where we are in life, this is a good question to ask ourselves: Which side of the equation am I on right now? And what should I do to be on the demand side?

Wise ones like Natarajan will always be in demand!

So, which side of the equation are YOU going to be on?

THE ROAD LESS TRAVELLED

Mr. Gururaghavendiran

IPCC – AIR 20 – Nov 2023

Miyamoto Musashi, Japan's most skilled swordsman ever, famously said, *"You must understand that there is more than one path to the top of the mountain!"* Thanks to his wise words, I've always known that there are a million ways to score a rank. So, I've never had a narrow, stereotypical view of it. But little did I imagine that college could prepare someone for a rank.

Just as Hogwarts School of Witchcraft and Wizardry shaped Harry Potter, Sri Sathya Sai Institute of Higher Learning prepared Gururaghavendiran for an All India Rank in his IPCC exams.

"I'm blessed to have studied in such a fine institution. The quality of education is extremely high, and they don't charge any college fee! It's a mandatory residential college, but even the hostel fee is very nominal. However, mobiles are prohibited, and they have a very strict routine. That routine disciplined me and prepared me for the CA preparations."

"I didn't attend classes for IPCC since 80 to 90 percent of the material was already covered in my B.Com. The quality of education was very good there, so I didn't really need classes. And, as I said earlier, my IPCC study routine was a lot easier than my college routine!" says Guru with a wide smile.

Here's how Gururaghavendiran's path to the top looked:

During the five months of preparation, he covered ICAI study modules once—highlighting the important points along the way. He watched free marathon revision videos on YouTube, and in the last month of his preparations, he wrote mock tests and worked out RTPs.

In his words, *"I invested 15 to 20 days for each subject, and I completed one subject at a time! I then had two revisions of 3–4 days each, per subject."*

When I asked him if he had any specific study methodology, he replied, *"While solving problems, I marked all the tough sums and the sums containing all adjustments, and I revisited those sums often. With regard to theory, it is better to use words and terminologies as in the study material; hence, I highlighted keywords and also used mnemonics to retain them!"*

Only those who have already reached the top of the mountain will know which paths will lead us there and which will lead us astray. So, I asked him, *"What is the most common mistake you see CA students committing?"*

His instant response was, *"Not giving enough importance to terminologies! Also, I'd advise my fellow student friends to study for knowledge rather than just for the exams. Ask, 'WHY is this provision this way?' and that will enhance your clarity."*

While trying to climb a mountain, it is only natural to stumble a few times. Guru had bad days too, and here's how he handled them: *"I'll tell myself that it is okay to have one or two bad days, but I'll always compensate later. And breaks are important too. So, it is really okay to take a break on your bad days!"*

"I had my fair share of fun! I used my mobile, went on walks with my mom, watched movies on weekends, and even went on pilgrimages. You can do all of that, as long as you plan your study accordingly!"

Life lesson: While climbing a mountain, it is okay to pause every now and then to admire the scenery around you. It is even important to do so. But we shouldn't get lost in that beauty and forget to keep climbing. The purpose of pausing is only to rest and rejuvenate so that we can climb more briskly and efficiently!

I am absolutely curious to know what pushed Guru to keep climbing. He replied, *"Fear of failure! If I didn't pass, I'd have to study the same thing again. This one thing pushed me to work harder each day!"*

Pro-tip: *Not all rank holders enjoy studying! More than one rank holder told me that they worked hard only to avoid repeating this process. So, whether you're driven by passion or fear, the trick is to keep climbing until you reach the top.*

The purpose of climbing a mountain is not to reside there forever; it is only to be able to see farther and find taller mountains to climb! Since Guru's next mountain is CA Final, I am genuinely curious. *"How confident are you of a rank in CA Final?"*

In an absolutely calm but confident tone, he says, *"I'm confident, sir! My exams are in November 2026, and I have already started preparing."* If you're wondering why so early, it is because Guru is pursuing his articleship at one of the Big 4 firms, and beginning early is the best way to ensure that work and studies don't impact each other adversely.

"But why did you choose the challenging path of the Big 4 while aspiring for a rank in CA Final?" I asked naively. After a minute of silent thought, he replied, *"We have to make time if we want to achieve big things. An articleship at the Big 4 strengthens your profile; many major companies prefer candidates with Big 4 articleship experience. It also provides an opportunity to work with ambitious, talented people."*

Maybe it isn't a coincidence that champions never choose the easy path. Or, maybe the tough path is what makes them champions!

And maybe that is why Robert Frost wrote:

I shall be telling this with a sigh
Somewhere ages and ages hence:
Two roads diverged in a wood, and
I took the one less travelled by,
And that has made all the difference!

<u>**Pleasure and Purpose**</u>

There once lived a bird that was too lazy to hunt for worms. So the bird struck a deal with a small boy who often played under the tree where the bird lived. "I'll give you one feather of mine for every five worms you bring!", said the bird and the boy happily agreed.

Every time the boy brought five worms, the bird would pluck one of its feathers to pay the boy. Very soon the bird lost all its feathers and it could neither pay the boy nor go and hunt!

This is precisely what happens when we trade our purpose for pleasure.

Have fun, enjoy life, but please ensure that your future isn't the price you pay for the present.

INSPIRATION

CA. Nandini Agrawal

Inspiring CA

CA Nandini Agrawal secured All India Rank 31 in her CA IPCC exams. Then, she secured All India Rank 1 in her CA Final exams and made it to the Guinness World Records as the world's youngest female Chartered Accountant for qualifying CA at just 19 years of age!

Here is the inspiring story of the enigma Nandini Agrawal, in her own words:

"I started schooling when I was 4. Bypassing nursery, I was enrolled directly in LKG and completed both LKG and UKG in one year. I then undertook a promotional test to be directly promoted to 2nd standard, and thereafter I was two years ahead of my peers. So when I got an All India Rank in my IPCC exams, an article appeared in the newspaper stating, 'Nandini Agrawal cleared CA Intermediate/IPCC at the age of 16.' That's when I realized I could create a world record by becoming a Chartered

Accountant at the age of 19! From that moment on, there was no looking back."

It is at this juncture that I realize I am interviewing a prodigy—the kind we label a *"born genius"!* And that's just the tip of an enormous iceberg. While most people might have rested on these mighty laurels for as long as possible, Nandini began using her fame and spotlight to inspire others toward greatness.

Nandini is now a powerful influencer, admired by the CA student community. So I asked her how that happened. Her candid response is:

"I began sharing my journey on the social media platform LinkedIn, and the response was great. The fact that both my brother and I cleared CA with All India Ranks—and my world record—brought a lot of attention to me. People encouraged me to continue writing, to create a YouTube channel, and to make my Instagram channel public. So I did all those things, and eventually I realized that I was doing something called 'content creation.' That's how the journey panned out."

Nandini is too wise to be carried away by fame. Her professional journey is as fruitful as her personal and social journey. She completed her articleship at PwC, then was placed at BCG upon qualifying as a CA, and after a 1.5-year stint there, she is now working as a Private Equity analyst.

Around a year ago, Nandini cleared all the exams of ACCA—a global organisation for professional accountants present in 179 countries. And she accomplished this the typical Nandini Agrawal way: with a World Rank of 7 (AIR 2) in the Strategic Business Reporting paper and a World Rank of 9 (AIR 3) in the Advanced Financial Management paper.

When I wondered how she manages to balance work and content creation, she explained that she owes it to her philosophy:

"Whenever you get time, do something toward your goal! It was more spontaneous than structured."

But her journey wasn't all hunky-dory, as some might presume. Some of her posts got mired in controversies, people judged her more by her age than by her wisdom, and some even commented on how she presented herself in front of the camera. Contrary to what many believe, rank-holders can't live on cloud nine forever. As Spider-Man's uncle once said, "With great power comes great responsibility!" Nandini had to prove to the world that she was worth her rank, her world record, and all her other credentials.

"She is too young and won't be able to handle the pressure of investment banking," said one recruiter. *I also heard remarks such as, "Although she has become a CA at such a young age, she won't be able to cope with corporate life," "She might have done a dummy articleship to secure AIR 1 at this age," and "She would have forged her birth certificate or faked her date of birth for the sake of fame!"*

All this noise affected me so much that I wasn't even able to focus on my interviews at the time. If I had allowed myself to be consumed by all that negativity, I would have lost it all! I told myself to keep focusing on my purpose with the same positivity as before and decided to channelize all my anger toward accomplishing something great.

"But where did you get the strength from?" I asked, and her one-word answer was, *"Purpose."*

When I requested her to elaborate, she said, *"My purpose is to help more and more people. It makes my day when someone tells me that I inspired them. I get immense joy out of helping people become successful—that's where I derive my strength."*

Realizing that Nandini is wiser beyond her years, I put aside my list of questions and began asking her some truly deep questions, all of which she answered beautifully.

"What drives you as a person?" I asked.

Her instant reply was:

"I am a spiritual person who reads books like The Bhagavad Gita and The Mahabharata. In the Mahabharata, when Arjuna was confused about whether to fight, Lord Krishna prodded him on, saying that as a Kshatriya, it was his duty to fight. So, I believe it is my duty to use my knowledge and skills for the welfare of those around me. This drives me to give my best every day."

She also draws her drive from her parents—especially her mother, who keeps reminding her that it is important to be independent—and from the ambitious people around her who are constantly hustling to accomplish big things in life.

Pro-tip: *A deep philosophy or purpose is the seed of greatness, and the people you surround yourself with are the soil in which that seed can flourish. If you get these right, it's all about watering the seed each day through consistent effort.*

Nandini also believes in the power of manifestation:

"Everything I've achieved in life, I've manifested at some point. Manifesting isn't goal-setting; in manifestation, you don't obsess over the details and timelines. You simply believe and do your best toward it."

Now that she has manifested these countless roles, I asked, *"How do you hone the skills needed to execute them so well?"* With a chuckle, she replied, *"In general, I am a very curious person. That helps me learn skills by talking to people, watching others do it, reading about it, and so on!"*

Since she mentioned reading, I asked her to recommend three books for my readers—and she named four. That's Nandini; she always gives more than she's asked for! Her book recommendations are:

1. *The Secret* by Rhonda Byrne
2. *Deep Work* by Cal Newport
3. *Siddhartha* by Hermann Hesse
4. *The Defining Decade* by Meg Jay

Nandini strongly reinforces my belief that reading makes you wiser beyond your years. Despite her hectic schedule, she manages to read at least one or two books each month!

Noticing how calm and composed she remained throughout the interview, I asked if she consciously works on her mindset. She said she is consistent with three practices:

1. I start my day with 10 minutes of positive affirmations.

2. During the day, I practice a mindfulness tool called *"traffic control,"* where I deliberately pause my thinking, bring my attention to my breath, and introspect on what really matters.

3. Before falling asleep, I think of everything for which I am grateful.

Almost every person who has attained greatness has daily rituals to keep themselves optimistic, grounded, and focused—and Nandini is no exception!

Though Nandini's crown of accomplishments is extremely heavy, she doesn't let even an ounce of that weight get to her. She's unassuming and candid when confessing her flaws and insecurities—a trait that comes only from someone who is truly comfortable in her own skin.

When I asked Nandini about her future plans, she confessed that she's at a crossroads right now. Curious about how she handles uncertainties and the accompanying confusion, she offered three pointers:

1. Talking to people helps you become aware of the options available.

2. Give it time rather than jumping into hasty decisions.

3. Set a timeline and do whatever makes the most sense to you at that juncture.

"One last question—what's your life philosophy?" I asked.

In a jiffy, she replied, *"Don't disturb others, and don't let others disturb you!"*

To me, Nandini's journey is a perfect example of how one should evolve over the years. She set a world record by securing All India Rank 1 and accomplished it in style. But now, she doesn't even know if her record has been broken—because she's no longer enamored by numbers. Just as a pole vaulter lets go of her pole upon soaring over the bar, Nandini has let go of her quest for personal greatness and is now focused on helping others attain greatness!

When you strive to win, you become an achiever;
when you strive to help others win, you become an inspiration!

UNTIL I WIN, I AM NOT DONE!

CA. Harish GC

AIR 47 – Final – Nov 2022

"Is it worth postponing my attempt in pursuit of a rank? I called Shashank frantically.

He assured me that a rank will open more doors than I even knew existed! Martin also validated that claim. So, I postponed my attempt, hustled hard, and scored a rank!"

(Both Shashank and Martin are rank holders featured in this book.)

Wow! While that sounds easy, taking such a huge risk is no joke! Where did the confidence come from, I wonder. Noticing my astonishment, he says, *"I was sure I was capable of an All India Rank. If they can, so can I!"*

To me, this is the perfect definition of the champion mindset! Whenever the storm of self-doubt blows your way, close your eyes, take a deep breath, and remind yourself: If they can, so can I! Harish swears by the power of visualisation. *"I pasted mark sheets of previous rank holders on my wall, and I constantly visualised my name on them. It worked wonders for me!"*

From Olympic athletes to multimillionaires, countless people vouch for the power of visualisation!

And most importantly, back that up with consistent effort: while a positive attitude may drive you to aim for the bullseye, it is your practice and effort that will decide whether you hit it or not! That's why Jim Rohn said, *"Discipline is the bridge between goals and accomplishments."*

Here are some boxes Harish ticked consistently:

1. One uninterrupted slot: Have at least one time slot when no one around is awake. This helps curb distractions and allows you to focus intensely.

2. Productive boredom: When you're bored or drained, solve past papers instead of wasting time.

3. Managing distractions: Whenever a distracting temptation pops into your mind, write it down. It gives you the satisfaction of having acknowledged it.

4. Concept clarity: Strive for 100% clarity on every concept.

5. Revision planning: Revising the entire syllabus in the one-and-a-half days between two exams is a huge challenge. Prepare a written plan in advance for those days.

6. Error tracking: Make a list of your errors (from your first study and initial revisions) and revisit them during the final lap of your revision. This will help you avoid repeating them in the exams.

Understanding my hunger for more, he continues:

"I'd also advise my juniors to take good care of their health! I fell ill during the last three exams, and I could barely breathe during the Direct Taxation

exam! I didn't study hard enough for the last paper because I felt I had already missed my chance at a rank. That's one regret I have. I should have pushed harder. If I had scored a little less, I would have missed the rank!"

Please don't get the wrong impression that Harish is a fragile soul who quits at the mere sight of a minor setback—that is not what champions are made of! Just two months before the examination, he suffered a major injury, yet he managed to push through and score a rank:

"With two months left for exams, I wanted to play football one last time and ended up injuring my leg. Two months of pain and bed rest affected my momentum. I truly regretted having ruined my preparations."

"So, how did you bounce back?" I interject curiously.

A few minutes of silence ensue. It seems Harish is reliving those moments of darkness. After a deep breath and a sigh, he says, *"It wasn't easy, sir! I told myself, 'Don't bother about things beyond your control.' I journaled my emotions to let them out, and I kept reminding myself that until I win, I am not done!"*

The words *"Until I win, I am not done"* keep ringing in my ears and tugging at my heart. I want to stay with those words for a little longer, but the clock is ticking and I have so much more to learn from this wise man. He speaks with passion and conviction, and like a true Chartered Accountant, he substantiates his claims with data. He passionately explains that awareness about an AIR and its benefits is very low in South India:

"In the North, students aim for a rank right from the start and structure their whole CA journey accordingly! Sadly, the awareness in the South is really low. We need to seriously create awareness here. Students need to start early and finish all classes at least six months before completing their articleship. Also, a rank in IPCC isn't as beneficial as a rank in Final—a rank in CA Final is a major deciding factor when it comes to your pay package. The starting package for rank holders

is extraordinary; it would take at least five to six years for others to catch up with that! And then there's the Management Development Programme."

The Management Development Programme is a two-week programme exclusively for rank holders, held at some of the finest management institutions like IIMs or ISB. This is a remarkable opportunity to learn from scholars at those institutions and to network with 49 other All India Rank holders.

"What more has rank done for you?" I ask. With a wide smile of satisfaction, he says, *"I've met some of the legends of our field, thanks to my rank, and the work exposure is immense!"*

Is a rank alone enough? Or are there more boxes to tick?

Pursuing articleship in one of the Big 4 firms can be a game changer, as some huge companies open their doors only to those with Big 4 exposure. Harish strongly recommends pursuing industrial training if you're considering a corporate career after qualifying as a CA.

So many boxes to tick and challenges to overcome sound overwhelming, don't they? Well, greatness doesn't come easy! Extraordinary grit and effort are the price you pay for it—and more often than not, you have to swim across oceans of negativity!

"A lot of people discouraged me! I wrote down their words on a notepad and referred back to it whenever I didn't feel like studying. That gave me the energy to push forward!"

After typing and deleting a dozen conclusions, I close my eyes to tap into the stillness within. In that canvas of silence, I see the image of a soldier atop a snowy mountain, standing firm amidst a fierce snowstorm! Harish is a soldier—a soldier who took risks, a soldier who fought life's battles fiercely, a soldier whose war cry is ***"Until I win, I am not done!"***

<u>RRR</u>

Success in the examination is a 3 step process:

1. Read
2. Revise
3. Recall

Read: is your first study where you read the textbook for concept clarity and to identify and memorise keywords. Once you've gained the concept clarity, you shouldn't have the need to revisit every sentence in the subsequent readings.

Revision: Revisit the keywords and key concepts of a chapter every now and then. Ideally, revise all previous chapters before beginning a new chapter. This is called 'Cumulative Revisions', and this is a real game-changer.

Recall: This where most CA students slip! Recall the keywords and key concepts of the portions covered, every now and then; and if you aren't able to recall, then quickly revisit those portions. But to be able to do this, you need to stop filling all your idle or free time slots with social media and gadgets. Recalling every now and then helps you cement what you've studied, while also keeping you tuned to the examination mindset.

A MILLION WAYS TO THE TOP

CA. H. Anantharaman

AIR 24 – CA Final – Nov 2024

Fascination for numbers led him to accounting, desire for respect brought him to Chartered Accountancy, and self-study earned him an All India Rank 24 in CA Final!

CA Anantharaman is the typical intelligent, school-topper type for whom Chartered Accountancy wasn't really a Mount Everest! But unlike many geniuses whose intelligence is accompanied by a tinge of pride—or even arrogance—Anantharaman wears humility as his crown!

Here is his story to greatness:

"I didn't start classes until I had completed one year of articleship. Thereafter, I tried watching free YouTube classes but found them very time-consuming. Hence, I decided to study on my own."

Before his study leave commenced, he had completed 90% of Financial Reporting and a little of every other subject. While he thought that an

AIR would be nice, he didn't consciously strive for it. *"The aim was only to cover 100% of the syllabus, to give my best! Likewise, I didn't focus on the number of hours—I focused on completing that day's portions, regardless of how long it took."*

Keeping things extremely simple and focusing on the basics is Anantharaman's style!

"I'd read every page of the book until I understood it, and only after understanding it would I move forward to the next page! And I linked the concepts of one subject with those of another. For example, I'd link a concept in Financial Reporting with a related concept in Advanced Financial Management; this helped deepen my clarity. I also linked the concepts I studied with the work performed in the office, wherever possible.

I'd also recommend following ICAI study materials. When it comes to the open-book exams (Integrated Business Solutions), the compilation of case studies doesn't help us answer questions in the exam hall. You may use it to practice, but do not rely on it for writing exams! ICAI study materials alone can help you write exams."

When I ask him what an *"AIR mindset"* is, he says that it is about focusing on covering 100% of the syllabus! In his opinion, if you're aiming for a rank, you can't afford to omit even the smallest of portions.

In addition to the above, sustaining that examination mindset is absolutely important! Anantharaman did this by using all non-study hours to recall the concepts he had studied. And whenever he couldn't recall something, he'd revisit those portions. This significantly improved his clarity and helped with retention.

And to go the extra mile, you need to keep yourself motivated. Anantharaman kept track of the ratio of pages completed versus pages pending, and these milestones kept him going.

"Even then, low days are inevitable. On such days, I'd study as much as I can, and the next day I'd forget about the previous day and focus on what can be done that day."

In addition, he'd often write his name with the prefix "CA" on a piece of paper and glance at it. While it might appear silly or even kiddish, such tiny acts remind us of our purpose and strengthen our resolve to pursue it relentlessly. *"The belief of people around me that I could achieve a rank also drove me to keep going,"* he adds.

Teaching, they say, is the best way of learning—and Anantharaman swears by this!

"One of my friends called me once a week to ask doubts, and I gained new perspectives while explaining to her."

As I mentioned earlier, keeping things simple is his style. Anantharaman didn't do remarkable things; he did simple things with remarkable consistency! He drew his confidence from his belief in God and built discipline and focus through his daily rituals. All of this, along with his inherently calm nature, helped him maintain composure when things didn't go his way in the exam hall. Needless to say, it also enhanced the overall quality of his mind and focus.

"I don't know if this is God's grace or some inexplicable magic; even in times when I was low on confidence or overthinking, when I started studying all other thoughts would vanish and I'd go into super-focus mode!"

Pro-tip: *Half the battle is always won or lost in the mind! So, along with your preparations, also work on your mind using tools like meditation, mindfulness, affirmations, visualisation, and so on.*

I know well that the fear of missing out (FOMO) can drive a person crazy and throw them off track. So I ask him if the fear of missing out on classes didn't affect him at all, and with that Buddha-like smile of his, he says:

"Sir, each one's path is different.
And there are a million ways to the top!"

THE BOOKLET GUY

CA. Amrut Deshmukh

Inspiring CA

I first met Amrut at a national-level conference for CA students in Coimbatore. Amrut and I were co-speakers, and I was also part of the organising committee. At 2:30 p.m. that day, I received a text from Amrut:

"Hey Shandip, has lunch been arranged at the venue? If not, please don't bother—I can go out for lunch."

Amidst the organising storms and chaos, the hospitality team had missed escorting the guest speaker for lunch! After arranging his lunch, when I apologised profusely, Amrut casually said, *"Shandip, I'm on a mission to make India read, period. My mission isn't to make India read while getting pampered; so, chill!"* I was blown away by his clarity and conviction!

And naturally, when I decided to interview inspiring Chartered Accountants for my book, the first name that came to mind was

CA Amrut Deshmukh—the man who has the wisdom to put his purpose ahead of petty egos!

Here's his journey, in his own words:

"Eight years ago, my first startup failed. Then my second startup failed. And then my third startup failed! In the process, 70% of my savings was wiped out! And just when I thought life couldn't get any worse, my relationship failed. Failure became such an integral part of my life that even my attempt to commit suicide failed!

During this extremely challenging phase, the universe decided to send me a message through my brother—a message that would change my life forever! 'Whenever you face a setback, read random. Don't read what you like; read what you need!' he said. And thankfully, even amidst this series of failures and setbacks, I didn't let go of my reading habit. Since books transformed my life, I became a social entrepreneur on a mission to make India read."

My curiosity overcame my fear of being judged, and I ended up asking him, *"Can you define social entrepreneurship, please?"* Amrut doesn't know how to judge; he only knows how to teach, inspire, and transform.

"A social entrepreneur is one who solves society's problems with compassion and empathy. While a social worker is at the mercy of donors, a social entrepreneur makes money to drive their own cause. I don't get money for my talks, but I'll ask them to give me a quality video of my talk."

Just as I was about to thank him for the clarity, he interjected with a strong reminder: *"Shandip, mindless growth is cancerous!"*

Amrut is a social entrepreneur who reads countless books and shares summaries of those books as audio clips via his mobile app. He has impacted countless lives through this novel initiative. His app, *"The Booklet Guy,"* has no advertisements, no subscription fee, and he doesn't seek donations either. To add to all of this, he doesn't even copyright his content!

"If making money isn't your objective, how do you sustain your lifestyle?" I ask. And the teacher in Amrut awakens once again:

"Frugality and miserliness are two very different things! I don't live by social standards or to impress people. I spend the money I save on what I value—health and books. I spend on avocados, quinoa, broccoli, and books—all of which people consider expensive."

I now wonder what triggered this phenomenal transformation, and Amrut says,

"A TED talk by a Pakistani social entrepreneur named Mr. Salman Khan transformed me. In his talk, he said that income sacrificed for the sake of society isn't a sacrifice; it is an investment in society. I then decided that I was going to donate my skills for the betterment of society, and I chose social media as the vehicle to drive my cause."

"I've heard that when you strive to do something for the world selflessly— the universe supports you in ways you can't even imagine! Is that true?" I ask.

"Undoubtedly," he roars. *"Shandip, my first book was pre-booked by over a thousand people, and even Amazon approached me saying they want to help me! When you give, give, and keep giving without any expectation, society will give you back ten times as much!"*

I am in complete awe, but I have miles to go before I can sit and process this overwhelming dose of inspiration! So, I shoot my next question: *"Only someone with a mighty purpose and absolute clarity about that purpose can be as inspiring as you are! So please tell me how to find one's purpose?"*

"You don't find your purpose by searching for it! You have to try many things, and when you connect the dots backwards, you'll find it along

the way. When you try many things, you'll at least know what not to do!"

Conversing with Amrut is like chatting with ChatGPT—there's simply no buffer time involved! He instantly dips his hand into his ocean of wisdom and pours a bucket of clarity on you! And just when you think he's done, another bucket of wisdom will hit you and overwhelm you! Here's the second bucket of wisdom:

"If your search is driven only by money, you'll never find your purpose! Once you find your purpose, fame and money will follow automatically, but happiness will become your intrinsic reward. The happiness you get from living your purpose will drive you to keep going. Thereafter, it's all about the journey and not the destination, and life becomes really beautiful!"

The greatest challenge in interviewing Amrut is that I so badly want to pause and ponder after every response of his, but time simply refuses to pause! Since his mission is all about reading and sharing summaries, I ask him how he manages to read so many books, and his eyes light up when he explains:

"I don't follow the academic style—which is to grab and retain as much as possible. I follow the elimination approach, where I eliminate all that I already know and all that I consider unimportant. But this comes from the experience of having read countless books."

Pro-tip: *In my own experience, after you've read a few dozen books, you'll be able to easily sift the important from the unimportant, the relevant from the irrelevant, and the core from the embellishments.*

"What about the subsequent process of note-taking?" I ask.

"Ah! Note-taking is an art! Most people write down the philosophy, and that is wrong. Our brain isn't designed to remember philosophies or quotes; it is the story that is important! Highlight or write down the story, and that

will help you remember the philosophy. So, just note down the stories and two or three big ideas from each book."

This is a true aha moment for me!

Lest I forget, Amrut is one of the fittest people I've ever come across! In other words, he's the only fit bookworm I've ever met! So, I ask where his passion for fitness comes from.

"My mission is to inspire the youth of our nation, and to do that, I have to look fit. I have to be someone they can look up to!"

Just as a compass keeps pointing north, every thought, word, and deed of Amrut points toward his purpose! He is 100% committed!

"And where does this commitment come from?" I ask. Amrut says it comes from the many touching experiences he has had. *"Please elaborate,"* I nudge, and he gladly recounts a touching experience:

"Once, a woman called me at odd hours of the night and praised my work for close to an hour! While I consider my work valuable, I found her praise greatly exaggerated. So, I bluntly asked her if she was trying to hit on me, and I was in tears when she said, 'Amrut, you have no clue how greatly you've impacted my life! I am a visually impaired person, but because of your audio summaries via your app, I wouldn't have had access to all the wisdom contained in those books. You've changed my life for the better, and I can never thank you enough!'"

Amrut is truly inspiring countless people through his work and who he is! Since it was books (and the gym) that shaped him into who he is today, I ask him for some topic-wise book recommendations, and he gladly obliges:

- On mindfulness: *Search Inside Yourself* by Chase Meng Tan
- On people skills: *Influence* by Robert Cialdini
- On health: *How Not to Die* by Michael Greger
- On purpose: *The Second Mountain* by David Brooks

- On happiness: *That Sounds Fun* by Annie F. Downs
- On relationships: *The Five Love Languages* by Gary Chapman
- On character: *Unposted Letter* by Mahatria
- On spirituality: *The Art of Happiness* by the Dalai Lama

"You've already shared so much, but can you share one last piece of advice for my readers?" I request. And he pours this last bucket of wisdom on me:

"Don't be obsessed with numbers; instead, focus on the unchangeable— basic human values that are timeless."

I often wonder if, just as Amrut wanted to summarise books, maybe the creator wanted to summarise values like integrity, compassion, and empathy—and so he created CA. Amrut Deshmukh!

<u>The Power of Purpose</u>

Does the name 'Lata Kare' ring a bell?

If not, it's high time you get to know about her!

Lata Bagavan Kare from Maharashtra first made headlines in 2013 when she ran her first marathon, barefoot and wearing a saree, at the age of 60. She ran neither for passion, nor for fame but for money! The marathon was her desperate attempt to arrange money for her husband's medical treatment.

Sharp stones pierced her feet, and the heat burned them; add to it the inconvenience of running a marathon in saree. But all this wasn't enough to stop her from winning the marathon!

The x-factor: A higher purpose!

While every other contestant ran for passion or fame, Lata Kare ran for the life of her husband. More than one rank holder featured in this book told me that wanting to make their parents proud was their driving force.

Want to make it big?

Find a purpose bigger than 'I', 'me' and 'myself'.

THE GO-GETTER

CA. Martin Vellanikaran

AIR 49 – IPCC – Nov 2018
AIR 46 – Final – Dec 2021

Go-getters don't wait for things to happen to them—they make things happen! Faith fuelled his takeoff, and determination kept him going.

"Balancing college and CA preparations wasn't easy. So, my studies were just good enough to pass. Out of the blue, I called my friend Shashank, and he gave me a 1-hour pep talk that changed everything—literally! It gave me the strength to study 12 to 14 hours a day!"

As he continues speaking, I quickly jot down in my notebook:

- Reaching out for help is important.

- Mentors who can guide and motivate are game-changers.

- There is no shortcut to success.
  (Mentors, motivators, or even God may brighten your path, but you have to walk it.)

Martin is not one to shy away from hard work. He's as much a hustler as he is a believer! He takes focus and effort very seriously—so seriously that he rented a room and moved in to avoid distractions!

"My game plan was simple: I attended one class at a time, did 2-3 revisions per paper, and wrote one test after each revision. The test series helped a lot. It is very important to analyse our test papers deeply, as that helped me see the outcome of my preparations and course-correct accordingly."

Pro-tip: One common trait among most rank holders is that they don't complicate the preparation process; they keep it absolutely simple so that consistency becomes easier.

Here are four study methods of Martin that earned him a rank:

1. Writing the formulas for FR and SFM in a separate notebook and revisiting them often.

2. Marking RTP questions in the main textbook and covering them soon after completing each chapter.

3. Using mnemonics while preparing for auditing.

4. The 5-highlighter method (my personal favourite).

The 5-highlighter method:

- During the 1st study: Highlight using a pen or pencil.

- During the 1st revision: Use a fluorescent highlighter for keywords, a pink highlighter for penalties and interest, and an orange highlighter for dates and numbers.

- During the 2nd revision: Use a dark green highlighter.

- In the 1.5 days between exams: Focus only on the dark green highlights.

And here are five pointers regarding exams:

1. Pray at least for a minute before your exams. It calms your mind and gives you confidence.

2. Use the 15-minute reading time very carefully to decide which questions to answer.

3. Aim to write for 100 marks and take plenty of tests to prepare yourself.

4. Please check your answer sheet before handing it over to the exam invigilator.

5. Do not discuss your answers with your friends until all the exams are over.

While most people are obsessed with doing, Martin is equally obsessed with being (the inner state of mind): "I gave up my smartphone not just to shut out distractions, but also to cut off peer pressure. Since I didn't have access to social media, I was totally unaware of what others were doing. And that eliminated all the needless peer pressure!"

"Even then, you would have had psychological challenges, right? How did you deal with them?" I ask doggedly.

His patient response is, *"Studying for long periods was indeed mentally challenging! Doubts like 'Am I going on the right track?' and 'What if I fail?' would nag from within. At such times, I'd remind myself that there's no time to worry! And if my emotional lows persist, I'd listen to a nice song or do something that would divert my mind and lift my spirits!"*

Pro-tip: *EVERY single rank holder I've interviewed for the book takes time very seriously!*

I am curious to know if, in retrospect, he has any regrets or if there is something he'd do differently if he had to do it all over again. With absolute conviction, he says, *"I had already given my 100%."*

This is precisely what makes these guys stand out: they give 100%—all the time! They don't stop until they know for sure that they've given it their all. That said, being practical is important; don't be too harsh on yourself. Martin, being a movie buff, rewarded himself with a movie whenever he completed a milestone. Use both the stick and the carrot to drive your mind toward your goal.

Martin wants me to share these two nuggets of wisdom with you:

- Please reach out to seniors or mentors who can guide you. Many times, we don't reach out because we don't want to disturb them—and they don't check on us for the same reason. These days, I reach out: I ask seniors for help and check on juniors.

- After succeeding, take a break, pause, and enjoy the moment. Celebrate your success.

As I pen this chapter under the star-studded sky, I wonder what Martin would be doing right now. Then I tell myself: he'd be hustling toward greatness. **That's what all go-getters do—they go the extra mile, ALWAYS!**

THE GOLDEN ARROW

CA. Simran Surana

AIR 36 – Final – May 2019

Kahlil Gibran used this beautiful metaphor for parents and children:

Parents are the bows from which children, as living arrows, are sent forth. The archer (the creator) bends the bow with all his might so that the arrows may go swift and far!

CA Simran Surana is the golden arrow that fulfilled the dream of two generations! Her grandfather wished to see his son (Simran's father) as a Chartered Accountant, but the arrow fell midway thanks to financial storms. Tides changed, the family grew financially, but Chartered Accountancy remained an unfulfilled dream. When Simran plunged into CA, the whole family was elated—they were confident that this arrow would certainly hit the target; but the bullseye was a shocker! AIR 36 was a pleasant surprise to the whole family, including Simran!

She says with absolute candidness, *"I genuinely didn't aim for a rank; I just didn't want to study these same books again. And I was willing to do anything and everything possible to circumvent that!"*

Both the desire for success and the fear of failure can be great motivators. The trick is to find what works for you. Find your driving force, use it to fuel your performance, and you too shall hit the target! But desire or fear without action amounts to nothing.

Simran began her CA Final preparations after one and a half years of articleship. She was also pursuing her B.Com back then, and juggling college, office, classes, and study wasn't a cakewalk. The full-time preparation phase wasn't easy either: *"Sitting still at one place was very challenging, and studying all alone within four walls was extremely depressing!"*

It was welcome news to me that not all AIRs enjoy the CA exam preparation rigmarole! But they persist because they're driven by purpose and not by emotions. As a case in point, Simran wasn't fond of theory papers and considered them her weak links—so she devoted double the time to them. She read them aloud, recorded them, and listened to them while walking and even while bathing! The plain truth is: if it is important to you, you'll find a way; if not, you'll find an excuse.

Hard work plus smart work helped her hit the bullseye. While people around were obsessed with scoring 50 or 60, Simran was obsessed with writing well for 100 marks. *"Complete the paper, answer all questions!"* she kept reminding herself. Her core belief is that aiming for a 60 will yield only 40; that is precisely why it is important to aim for an 80 or 90. More importantly, aim to write well for 100 marks!

Simran says her x-factor, however, was creating notes on A4 sheets! She confined an entire chapter to one sheet, which enabled her to revise easily and thoroughly in the one and a half days between two exams. As Shiv Khera famously said, *"Winners don't do different things, they do things differently."*

More than one rank holder told me this: *"People think rank-holders know it all and get everything right. No, we don't! We make mistakes too."* Simran's biggest mistakes, in her own words, were not practicing enough sums in costing due to overconfidence and wasting a lot of time dwelling on regret after her Financial Reporting exam didn't go as planned.

Her advice for students is: *"Don't even check if your answers are right. What's done is done, and can't be changed. So don't waste the precious one and a half days in checking, regretting, and worrying!"*

If, like me, you are wondering how she hit the bullseye despite these costly mistakes, well, she got a lot of other stuff right! Just as an arrow traveling toward a target doesn't sway an inch from its trajectory, she didn't let any distraction divert her from her preparation. No smartphone, no outside food, and a disabled cable connection (for the entire family—they wanted a CA, right?).

She says, *"It was not at all easy, but it was absolutely worth it! The satisfaction of settling well in life and the happiness of seeing our parents proud makes everything worth doing!"*

Simran educates me that most PSUs and many mighty MNCs hire only All India Rank holders. After a successful stint at Indian Oil Corporation Limited, she has now set up her own office in Mumbai.

"No partners?" I ask curiously, and she says she doesn't know too many people in Mumbai since she's quite new to the place. How, then, did she set up an office in unknown territory? *"That's the confidence an AIR gives! If I could do that, I can do anything!"* are her concluding words—and she says this without even an iota of arrogance.

After fulfilling her family's dreams, she is now striving toward her own. In this new chapter of life, she is both the golden arrow and the bow that fires it!

Fun Theory

In the early 2000s, Volkswagen conducted a series of experiments where they made modifications to make mundane things interesting. The first activity, the Piano staircase, took place in Stockholm subway, where they installed piano keys on the staircase. The goal was to try and make more people use the staircase.

And guess what?

The results were astonishingly significant! Up to 66% people now took the staircase!

In another experiment, the company tried to increase the number of people that were throwing waste in trash cans. They did this with the help of technology, by adding sensors and voices to trash cans. Whenever someone put something into the trash can, the can would make a whooshing and crashing sound. More and more people began gathering around these trash cans for the fun of these sounds. And an enormous amount of trash was collected compared to before!

The 'Fun theory' states that the best way to accomplish something is to turn it into fun!

So, if you want to score a rank, look for ways to turn your studies into fun!

IF I CAN, SO CAN YOU!

CA. Omkar Jayant Nirgudkar

Inspiring CA

The neighbours said, *"Don't educate him; just set up a telephone booth for him."*

His friends said, *"Don't worry, we'll take care of you."*

Omkar said, *"No thanks, I can take care of myself,"* and he qualified CA and CS!

Omkar's life is nothing short of an inspiring blockbuster—the first half whispers *"I can,"* and the second half screams *"so can you!"*

Omkar was diagnosed with cerebral palsy at the tender age of four! His first challenge was attending a normal school, and his parents had to fight hard for even this basic right. The municipal school administration denied him admission, saying they did not have the human resources to care for a differently-abled child. He was finally allowed to join after his parents promised that one of them would wait outside the classroom during school hours to take care of him. *"For four years, my mom sat outside my classroom! Then the teachers gained the confidence that I'd manage on my own."*

Everyone around ridiculed my parents for enduring so much hardship to educate me. *"Focus on your other child, and he will take care of Omkar!"* they said. Some even asked my parents to set up a telephone booth for me. But, thankfully, my parents were persistent in educating me!

The positive side of studying in a municipal school was that the children there didn't have a superiority complex and treated me as an equal. I wasn't treated as a special child; they included me in everything they did. I couldn't play, but they wouldn't begin the game until I went and sat on the ground as an audience—a situation that was very conducive to my mental growth.

One common thread I noticed in the journeys of all differently-abled people is that they had to fight long and hard for even the most basic rights and privileges that we enjoy on a daily basis. Omkar wasn't allowed to attend the carpentry class in school because the teacher feared that he might hurt himself. *"My father asked the teacher what he'd do if the other kids got injured. When the teacher said he'd rush them to the hospital, my father requested him to do the same for me. Sadly, he refused. And for the first time, I felt different."* (Omkar said "different," not "lesser"—that is Omkar for you!)

"What exactly did you tell yourself in those moments?" I ask with concern. *"I told myself, 'If I stop here, the situation wins. But if I keep going forward, I win!'"*

In college, Omkar gained access to a huge library, and that's where he began growing his wings of knowledge. Alongside that, he was also busy contributing to society in other ways—like donating blood (he has donated blood 64 times!), organising blood donation camps, compèring for social events, and donating small amounts of money to social causes.

This is when he bumped into a Chartered Accountant who promised him an apprenticeship slot if he plunged into CA. But life wasn't done testing him! *"My spasticity increased, and I had to undergo surgeries on my legs. So, I had to study from home. I took a few attempts, but eventually passed and joined articleship. And for the first time, I was respected for my work—not my disability!"*

"What were some challenges you faced as a CA student?" I ask. *"My disability restricted my movements, so I couldn't create a study circle for myself. Hailing from a remote city meant there were no coaching classes. Additionally, I had to put in extra effort since I'm not inherently intelligent!"*

But I overcame all odds and qualified CA in 2011. In the meantime, I also cleared CS and M.Com. I am the first person in India to clear both CA and CS despite being affected by cerebral palsy! Now, I had to translate my educational qualifications into tangible income.

My friends said, *"Don't worry, we'll take care of you,"* and that stung me hard! I told myself, *"Why should anyone take care of me? I will take care of myself!"* and I went for campus placement.

I was selected by six companies—including some Big 4 firms and other prestigious companies. I selected HPCL. I want to stress that I had the luxury of choice because differently-abled people usually don't get that opportunity! I was part of the ERP department—which was an intellectually challenging job. I earned my promotions like any normal person and did not claim any advantages for being differently abled.

No matter how hard life tried to break and confine him, he broke all shackles and soared higher and higher! Finally, nature decided to give up, surrender, and acknowledge his relentlessness and positivity! Omkar was honoured with the *"National Award for Best Employee (Cerebral Palsy)"* in 2013 by the then Honourable President of India, Shri Pranab Mukherjee!

"You're settled now, you're excelling professionally, you've won so many awards, you've done it all. What drives you now?" I ask.

"Empowering disabled people!" he says with a smile that holds traces of both pain and pride!

"Any words of advice for students?" I ask, trying to pull him out of the intense emotions he's experiencing.

"Sure! I have three pointers," he says, and shares these:

- Limit your social media usage—it will most certainly distract you.

- Learn from your failures.

- Be consistent in your efforts.

Despite all that life put him through, Omkar doesn't harbor any bitterness. *"My life is a mixed package; I've faced my fair share of good and bad. People have come out of nowhere and helped me, and people have also harmed me for no reason. I believe in karma, so I guess I get only what is due!"*

Now, trying to pull myself out of the intense emotions I'm experiencing, I shoot my next question: *"Where does your motivation come from?"*

And with a childlike smile, Omkar says, *"From my parents! When they didn't give up on me, how can I?"*

I met Omkar for the first time at a national-level conference for CA students in Coimbatore. As he stood on the stage after the session, with his co-panelists, the entire auditorium gave him a standing ovation. And he roared, ***"If I can, so can you!"***

SELF-MADE!

CA. Ghilman Saalim Ansari

AIR 3 – Final – May 2024

Have you heard of someone who qualified CA without the help of coaching classes? I haven't. To be precise, I hadn't—until I came across CA Ghilman Saalim Ansari. He didn't just qualify CA; he hit the ball straight out of the park and secured All India Rank 3! How's that for inspiration?

Ghilman didn't enter CA thinking he'd score a rank:

"When I got in, I didn't even think I'd clear on the first attempt! I thought I'd clear in 3 to 4 attempts, and that would be okay."

Now I'm curious where the AIR aspiration came from. Ghilman explains,

"After coming to CA Final, I realised that if I work for a rank, I don't have to worry about passing or failing. An All India Rank would open new doors for me—so I aspired for a rank."

"But how did you even manage without classes?" I wonder aloud. Wisdom never screams in pride. Without any airs of accomplishment, Ghilman explains,

"Once you understand the concept, application becomes easier. YouTube videos helped me grasp the concepts. In my opinion, much of your results depend on the quality of your self-study. In Foundation and in IPCC, I checked with my friends to see if I got the concepts right; in Final, I was confident."

With a lot of hesitation, I ask if he opted for self-study for financial reasons.

"No!" he says with a smile. *"When I inquired about classes, they said they'd be full-day classes spanning 6–8 hours. I can't sit for that long—I lose focus after 30 minutes. So, I chose self-study."*

Pro-tip: *If you lack self-discipline, it is better to go for classes. Self-study demands extraordinary self-discipline.*

So, I am naturally curious about his daily habits:

"I woke up early each morning and studied for around 12 hours a day. I kept increasing this number, and during the last month I would clock around 14–16 hours a day!"

Sensing my astonishment, he continues,

"I had only one thing in mind: If I don't clear this time, I will have to repeat this grueling process!"

"But how did you handle emotional lows without any external support system?" I ask. After a brief silence, Ghilman clears his throat and says,

"I told myself that hope is important and I can't afford to lose it! I also knew that forgetting what we've studied happens to everybody. With increased efforts through revisions and recall, I can overcome that. I also spent time with family and friends to replenish myself."

"And what about FOMO (the Fear Of Missing Out)?" I leap curiously.

"It is normal to have that. I told myself that it is only a matter of time and I'll join them soon."

Ghilman is certainly cut from a different cloth! He has absolute clarity about his strengths, weaknesses, aspirations, and challenges. I've seen people with clarity, but the depth and strength of his were truly outstanding!

"Can you tell me what an AIR mindset is?" I ask, awaiting an outpouring of clarity.

"Give your 100%. Cover 100% of the portions. You can't omit something just because you don't understand it. Increase your efforts, and never lose hope!" he roars.

When I ask him what his biggest learnings in this journey were, he shares three lessons:

- Hard work always pays off.
- Consistency is the key.
- If you enjoy what you do, you'll be able to do it well.

I carefully jot down every word he utters—each coming from his own experience. This is what makes conversations with self-made people priceless.

According to him, the single biggest mistakes CA students make are naively assuming that classes can substitute for self-study and neglecting writing practice.

Pro-tip: *Ghilman recommends writing multiple mock tests because they help you assess your progress while giving you adequate writing practice.*

When I ask him to share one piece of advice for my readers, he sums it up in two words: *"BE CONSISTENT!"*

"One last question: has an AIR made you more confident?" I ask with a probing look.

"I was confident even before exams," he replies without batting an eyelid. This is what winners are made of!

"If you can dream it, you can do it," said Walt Disney. You need enormous confidence to dream big and truckloads of courage to pursue it all alone. In other words, you need to become your own version of CA Ghilman Saalim Ansari!

<u>Keep Going</u>

Once two frogs fell into a large milk pot. The first frog gave up after sometime, slowly sank and died. The second frog resolved to keep trying until the last ounce of its energy. As the second frog kept flapping its legs, the milk got churned and gradually a ball of butter began forming.

The butter grew bigger and bigger with time, and soon the ball of butter was big enough for the frog to climb on, and leap out of the pot!

As someone who has been mentoring students for over a decade, one common mistake I see students committing is wasting precious time in anxiety or regret.

When you are at crossroads, and are clueless about what to do, idling away time in indecision is not the wise choice. When you don't know what to do, please do something!

Pro-tip: *Clarity doesn't come from waiting, it comes from doing.*

THERE ARE NO ACCIDENTS

Mr. Vigneshwar

AIR 26 – Foundation – Nov 2019

Master Oogway, the wise old teacher in the movie *Kung Fu Panda*, was fond of reminding those around him, *"There are no accidents!"* He said it so often that his pupil Shifu annoyedly reminded him, *"You've already said that twice."* To that, Oogway replied with a smile, *"That was no accident either!"*

Vigneshwar is no different:

"Nothing happens by accident. The All India Rank 26 wasn't a fluke—almost everything was pre-planned! Meticulous planning backed by consistent efforts gave me the rank. There are no accidents!"

He says this with a calm confidence that reminds me of the legendary teacher, Master Oogway.

A school topper in his 10th and 12th standards, Vigneshwar chose CA thanks to the guidance of his school principal. *"Yet another rule-book story of a studious kid who excelled in studies,"* I think to myself. As if reading my mind, he says, *"Sir, I was just another playful kid who enjoyed the pleasures of childhood until I lost my father when I was 7. Thereafter, life took a U-turn. I had to relocate to my mother's native place and join a new school. Life wasn't easy."*

It seems Kahlil Gibran was indeed right when he said, *"Out of suffering have emerged the strongest souls. The most massive characters are seared with scars!"* Even after all these trials and tribulations, if someone can believe that there are no accidents, then an All India Rank is not a mighty feat at all!

Aspiring for greatness is the easy part; striving for it consistently and persisting in the face of adversities is the real test. Vigneshwar's preparations spanned six months—four months of classes and study, and two months of revision. Hailing from a suburb, he had to endure a 2 – to 3-hour bus commute each day to attend classes at a good academy. This meant having to study even on the bus in order to achieve his target of 10–12 effective hours per day. Certainly, success doesn't come easy!

Even as I'm trying to process this, he says, *"The CA Foundation journey actually felt effortless, thanks to my even more rigorous 14-hour school routine!"* Getting accustomed to and comfortable with a rigorous routine is the first step to greatness.

He says that three factors earned him a rank:

1. Being persistent about achieving 100% clarity.
2. Frequent revisions using new types of sums and case studies.
3. Keeping his study methods simple and consistent.

Having scored a rank in Foundation, it was only natural for Vigneshwar to aspire for a rank in his Intermediate exams. But life has its strange ways of throwing us off balance and challenging us to bounce back. COVID and the demise of his dear grandfather—who was also a mentor—threw him off track. So, Vigneshwar postponed his attempt by six months and prepared thoroughly for a rank, yet he missed an AIR by a meagre 3 marks!

"Do you regret having postponed your attempt?" I ask, and without batting an eyelid he replies, *"Not at all, sir! I'm only glad that I aimed high and didn't settle for less."*

Even before I can recover from my awe, he continues, *"Sir, if I can't go back and do something again, I do it only when I can give my 200% effort! Even now, I am eligible to write my CA Final exams in November 2024, but I have postponed them to May 2025 so that I can give my 200%. If I write my final exams now, I know well that I will succeed— but if I miss an AIR, they will not allow me to rewrite the exams for a rank!"*

Is this what Steve Jobs meant when he said, *"Stay hungry, stay foolish?"* I wonder.

Here are some nuggets of wisdom from this young Oogway:

Q: *Now that you've postponed your attempt, how confident are you of scoring a rank?*

> A: *I'm 100% confident! I'm not saying this out of an adrenaline rush— I'm saying this out of the confidence I have in my consistent efforts and persistence!*

Q: *Fabulous! I am curious to know why you agreed to this interview in the first place?*

> A: *The universe has given me so much; for the first time, I've gotten an opportunity to give back. I am an arrow, and I need a bow to reach the target! I felt you are the perfect bow to take my knowledge to the student community.*

> *(Every response of his only increases my love and admiration for this guy.)*

Q: *What is an AIR mindset?*

> A: *Persistence—never giving up (and he stresses the words "at all"). While others are okay with skipping or losing 10–20 marks, we realise the importance of every single mark. There is a huge difference between 99 and 100! And, of course, consistency; continuing our preparation even when we don't have the motivation.*

Again—persistence and consistency! I even consider reminding him that he has already said it twice. He would probably remind me that this was no accident either!

Wondering if I am overwhelmed, he reassures, *"It is not all that difficult if you retain only the top-priority items on your to-do list and ruthlessly cut out everything else. Then you only have a handful of tasks to focus on, and consistency becomes easier."*

Q: *What's your favourite movie and why?*

> A: *Bahubali and KGF. In both of these movies, the hero is an ordinary person with an audacious goal. And when they strive with persistence, the whole universe helps them succeed!*

The psychologist in me can't help wondering if Vigneshwar sees himself in these protagonists because both lost a parent at their tender age!

Q: *Even the Bahubalis and the Rockys can have bad days, right? How do you handle those low days?*

> A: *While my roof is limitless, my floor is always fixed and cemented! On bad days, I make sure I tick at least the bare minimum portions.*

Assuming he has completed the answer, I begin shooting the next question when he interjects, *"And I make up for the lag by being extraordinary the next day!"*

This guy is a totally different package! Well, all rank holders are!

And that's precisely WHY I wrote this book—to find out how different these people are from the rest of us, to understand what makes them different, and to decode how they achieved greatness!

This book isn't meant to tell you that they are extraordinary while you are ordinary. It is meant to remind you that you too can become extraordinary by going the extra mile—like they did, and will always do!

But please remember: **there are no accidents!**

BREAK THE WALL

CA. AL Alagammai

AIR 29 – Final – Nov 2019

"When your back is against the wall, break the goddamn thing down!"
— Harvey Specter, the protagonist of the renowned series *Suits*

And Alagammai literally lived that mantra to score her rank!

Alagammai wasn't a state topper, district topper, school topper, or even a class topper. She failed once in the CA Foundation, once in the CA IPCC exams, and once in the CA Final exams—and then decided she'd had enough of mediocrity in life. So she hustled extremely hard for two months and scored All India Rank 29 in her CA Final exams! One strong decision and two months of incredible effort were all she needed to turn her life around. It seems true that we're always only one decision away from greatness.

"I feared blood, so pursuing medicine was out of the question. I was never inclined toward engineering, so commerce was the only choice remaining.

When I googled Chartered Accountancy, I learnt that I'd get to be my own boss if I became a Chartered Accountant—and that enticed me to take the plunge."

An ordinary start, right? Everything beyond this would be extraordinary! So, please brace yourselves!

"After 10 months of preparation, I failed my first attempt at the CA Final exams. This added to the baggage of past failures, dented my self-confidence and self-esteem, and I slipped into depression. Thanks to elections, the May 2019 exams had been postponed by a month, and I now had only 60 days for my November 2019 exams, as against the usual three months—so I had to race against time to complete the vast syllabus in hand. I analysed my failure and realised that I hadn't revised enough in the first attempt. My friend Nandini (who had also failed in the last exam) and I studied together, pushing each other to give our absolute best. She secured AIR 27, while I got AIR 29! It was she who nudged me (two hours after the results were out) to check the merit list—and only then did I know that I had scored an All India Rank!"

"Considering the vastness of the syllabus, what did you even focus on during those two months?" I gasp.

"My sole focus was on being able to revise an entire subject in one day and recall it in three hours—so that I could revise effectively in that one day between two exams and recall effectively during the three-hour examinations."

Pro-tip: *Speed helps only when you're running in the right direction. Always begin with the end in mind. For every task or goal in life, define the end goal clearly and work backward to arrive at your daily to-dos.*

"Did you aim for an All India Rank?" I ask naively.

"Yes, but I wasn't obsessed with it. The idea was to aim for a rank so that I'd at least pass!"

But to accomplish such a remarkable feat in just 60 days, she must have checked many boxes! So I ask her which study methods helped her secure her rank, and she lists three:

1. Following ICAI study material: Most authors tend to shorten the volume; as a downside, they remove at least 30% of the content—so we study only 70% of the material, and out of that 70%, we end up forgetting around 20%.

2. Belief in the power of self-study: No matter where you attend classes, in the end, it's all about how effectively you study.

3. Not missing out on Revision Test Papers and Mock Test Papers.

Pro-tip: *Most people wrongly assume that smart work is all about taking shortcuts! Contrary to popular belief, the really smart ones refrain from shortcuts—they take the arduous path to perfection!*

"So, how exactly did the 60 days go?" I ask.

After a laugh, she replies, *"I kept track of the days—like they do in the TV programme Big Boss: Day 1, Day 2, Day 3, Day 4, and so on. Other than the time spent on daily chores and one hour of watching Big Boss for relaxation, every other waking hour was devoted to studies! I clocked 12 to 14 effective hours each day, and that momentum translated into results!"*

Alagammai even used her leisure time to recall portions of various subjects. This was the real game changer, as it helped her not only retain the concepts but also stay in that exam mindset.

Pro-tip: *Tuning into and staying rooted in that exam mindset is what truly determines the quality of your performance.*

Another X-factor in Alagammai's 60-day sprint was having an equally determined study buddy.

"We sat for each other!" she says with immense satisfaction.

Though a short span like two months doesn't give you much scope to strategise, Alagammai had strategies in place wherever possible. She planned the 1.5 days between exams well in advance. *"The evenings after exams were reserved for easy chapters. I'd tackle the big and complex chapters the next morning, and that evening was reserved for the easiest or simplest chapters. On the day of the exam, I'd do an overall revision and stop studying at 10:00 a.m.—though I'd continue recalling everything I'd studied in that subject."*

Alagammai lists self-made notes and frequent revisions as the two strongest pillars of her two-month success story.

Elaborate strategies and exhaustive techniques are possible only when you begin early and work consistently—and you can very well pick them up from any of the other All India Rank holders featured in this book. From Alagammai, I'd like you to take one thing to heart: when the odds are against you, when life pushes you against the wall—break the goddamn thing down, and keep moving! That is the way to greatness!

<u>Where Did I Go Wrong?</u>

The legendary basketball player Kobe Bryant once missed a deciding shot in the last few minutes of the game. And that missed shot cost his team the trophy! And Kobe Bryant was seen sitting with his head hung low, and his palms covering his face.

Half an hour later, as he was exiting the stadium, a journalist asked him, "Kobe you appeared very upset! What emotions were you processing?"

And Kobe Bryant roared, "What does it have to do with emotions? I was analysing how I missed the shot! Now that I know where I went wrong, I can work on it!"

As a student, I've wasted countless days feeling low! And that is one of my biggest regrets!

When you falter, when you have a bad day, or when nothing seems to be going into your head: don't allow that to translate into a bad mood! Instead, like Kobe Bryant, close your eyes and analyse what's impacting you! And you can bounce back stronger! That's how legends are made!

PURSUIT OF HAPPINESS

CA. Isha Verma

Inspiring CA

CA Isha Verma is a Chartered Accountant working as a business analyst in the banking sector. As a hobby, she posts videos that inspire and inform CA students, and countless people have benefited from those videos.

A Kathak dancer since the age of five, Isha began posting her dance videos on YouTube in 2015 with the sole intent of sharing them with her loved ones. Since WhatsApp didn't support large files, she had no choice but to upload them on YouTube. What began as a necessity metamorphosed into a passion during the COVID-19 pandemic.

"Being confined to my house made my CA Final preparation journey all the more stressful. So I felt it would be nice to continue my passion for dancing and share those videos on YouTube. Though I loved the process of shooting and posting videos, dancing required makeup, good costumes, an

aesthetic background, etc., and this was extremely challenging. So I created another YouTube channel where I began sharing CA-related videos. All I needed was a camera, and I could present myself the way I am!"

"But what was the driving force to keep going?" I ask.

Isha Verma explains that even as a student, she used to promote ICAI events and other programmes relevant to CA students on her social media profile. *"I once participated in an elocution competition as part of the Talent Hunt Programme held at the branch, regional, and national levels. I posted a live vlog of the entire event—my preparation and everything—and the response was great. It was then that I realised YouTube was a great way to keep my fellow CA student friends informed about the various opportunities available to them. The fact that my videos help a lot of people is what keeps me going!"*

Pro-tip: *When your purpose extends beyond yourself, you go from being a winner to becoming a leader!*

In a world hankering after subscribers, likes, and comments, Isha posts videos solely because she loves the process of shooting and sharing them. *"I needed a break from studies, so I did this. None of my videos ever went viral, and the subscribers grew organically over the years. I'm happy doing this, and people benefit from it—that's all that matters."*

To an outsider, the job of a social media influencer might appear easy, but that is far from the truth. *"I faced a lot of judgments, especially before I qualified. When I failed, many people said I was failing only because of YouTube. At the same time, the support I received was also huge! A lot of people appreciated me for doing something different. And thankfully, I qualified as a CA."*

When I ask her how she handled baseless criticisms and hate comments, she says it doesn't affect her anymore, thanks to her clarity about her purpose. *"I don't even block them or react to their comments; if that gives them happiness, then so be it,"* she says with a laugh, showing that she doesn't harbor even a wee bit of anger or hatred toward her critics.

I've always believed that any work done passionately transforms us in the long run. So I was interested in knowing how her work has transformed her as a person. *"I am a huge introvert! The process of shooting videos has made me comfortable interacting with people, and my self-confidence has grown over the years. If I'm sounding confident now, I owe it to those videos."*

And it is those videos that have given CA Isha Verma an identity! She now serves as a judge or a keynote speaker at the very same student conferences where she once presented papers as a student. While this makes her happy, her satisfaction comes from the many messages of gratitude she receives from CA students thanking her for helping them succeed—or even transform.

And just because this is a hobby, she doesn't take it lightly! She's extremely passionate about it. *"There are still a lot of myths and confusion about many aspects of the CA preparation journey. Clarity is the need of the hour, and if my videos help them gain that clarity even in a small way, I'm happy about it. I feel good when I contribute meaningfully!"*

Pro-tip: *If you want to feel good, contribute meaningfully to the well-being of those around you.*

Since many people are interested in content creation these days, I asked her for some gyaan on the subject, and she said:

1. Start! Only then will you know if you really enjoy doing it.

2. Do it not for the traction (likes, comments, subscribers, etc.) but solely because you love it!

Her advice for CA students is also to focus on other areas of self-development along with their studies. *"There's always time that we waste—use that time for this!"*

Isha didn't pursue greatness; she only pursued happiness!

When you pursue happiness not just for yourself but for others too, greatness is thrust upon you!

THAT'S HOW WINNING IS DONE!

CA. Ajay

AIR 39 – Inter – May 2019
AIR 36 – Final – May 2022

Some people remind us of our favourite memories—we never know why! Ajay keeps reminding me of my favourite movie quote from the Hollywood classic *Rocky*:

"You, me, or nobody is going to hit as hard as life. But it ain't about how hard you hit. It's about how hard you can get hit and keep moving forward. That's how winning is done!"

That is precisely how CA Ajay achieved his success! Life kept knocking him down, and he kept getting back up—stronger than before!

Two months before his CA Intermediate exams, Ajay fell ill; and two months before his CA Final exams, his parents were down with COVID. COVID brought with it a plethora of uncertainties and challenges.

"How then did you manage to score an All India Rank amidst all this chaos?" I wonder aloud.

Ajay answers in a calm and composed tone, *"It's all about adaptability. You've got to see the positives. Eliminate the negatives in the situation and focus only on the positives!"*

The beauty is that he did not even aim for a rank!

"I didn't want to pressurise myself. I didn't even do anything special to score a rank. I simply gave my best—that's all! But routines are important: eating habits, sleep, and what you do to relax—all of that counts. Occasional relaxation is okay."

I wonder if he's talking about CA or boxing! Both CA and boxing are really about conquering ourselves; in this process, our mind can be our greatest ally or our toughest opponent.

So, how did this champion really prepare for his bout?

"I used a diversified method:

- *I'd study at least three subjects a day—one practical, one theory, and one tax paper.*
- *Each three-hour slot was divided into four segments:*
    - *The first 30 minutes: to revise previous portions.*
    - *The next 90 minutes: to study new portions.*
    - *The following 30 minutes: to solve questions.*
    - *The final 30 minutes: to write down notes.*

And for theory papers (especially audit), I converted concepts into questions so that I wouldn't be confused about which answer to match with which question."

Most students face this challenge in auditing, which is why many auditing question papers appear very general. This method of converting concepts to questions can be a real game changer for theory papers. Want audit evidence? This strategy helped Ajay score 89 in CA Intermediate and 82 in CA Final auditing papers.

For his CA Final, Ajay prepared for about eight to nine months. *"I didn't push hard initially. However, I recorded the time I studied and then focused on improving it. Eventually, I was clocking over 12 hours a day on a consistent basis."*

Pro-tip: *Only what gets measured gets accomplished!*

Since he is now a teacher, I asked him for some tips on how to utilise classes better, and here's what he says:

"Classes are just to help you understand or enhance your understanding. They aren't a substitute for self-study; they're only supplements to enhance the quality of your first study. So, recollect on the same day itself. Preparation is a three-step process:

1. *Understand*

2. *Analyse*

3. *Study*

Classes will help you with the first two steps, but you have to walk the third step by yourself!"

When I ask him how he handled his low days, he says, *"I'd imagine that tomorrow is my result day—that'll give me the drive to push harder."* I couldn't help thinking, *"No wonder this man reminds me of Rocky Balboa; he's more a boxer than a CA!"*

Ajay's advice for students is:

"Do what you have to do today—properly. Direction, intensity, and consistency are absolutely important. Life may throw a lot of obstacles on your path, but you shouldn't let them affect your direction, intensity, or

consistency. If your intentions and efforts are genuine, nothing can ever stop you."

Always remember: **that's how winning is done!**

<u>Hope is a Good Thing</u>

Psychologist Kurt Richter conducted an experiment with wild rats. He put 5 wild rats into a large drum of water and timed how long they survived. He repeated this experiment Plenty of times with different bunches of rats, and invariably they all averaged 15 minutes, after which they gave up, sank and died!

He then introduced a change to the experiment. At the 10th minute, he would pull out the rats, and wrap them in a ball of towel to give them warmth and comfort. Once their vitals returned to normal, he'd throw them into the drum of water once again.

This time guess how long the rats managed to stay afloat?

They averaged 60 hours!

Yes, you read it right! 60 hours!

That's a whopping 240 times the initial average of 15 minutes!

The magical element?

HOPE!

Once they were rescued at the 15th minute, they developed the hope that if they survived a little longer, some external force would come and rescue them! And this hope caused them to keep striving!

As the protagonist of the classic movie Shawshank Redemption, Andy Dufresne says, "Always remember: Hope is a good thing, maybe the best of things, and no good thing ever dies!"

Never lose hope! Never!!!

CHALLENGE ACCEPTED

CA. Chinmay Bengani

AIR 2 – Foundation – Nov 2020
AIR 29 – Final – Nov 2024

Like most people, Chinmay chose Chartered Accountancy for the respect it garners. Since the decision was made even before he completed his 12th grade, he plunged directly into CA without pursuing an undergraduate degree.

"Thanks to COVID, recorded classes were the only choice, and quickly adapting to that mode of learning was a mighty challenge. But the advantage was that I could decide the timings and pace of the classes. The guidance of my teachers, when combined with my efforts, gave me an All India Rank 2 in the CA Foundation examination. Unfortunately, that mindset changed; I became lethargic and, most naturally, I didn't score a rank in CA Intermediate."

But Chinmay's glory lies not in never falling but in rising every time he falls! He resolved to make up for his failure, picked himself up, and plodded on with faith and pluck.

"I began my CA Final preparations exactly after one year of articleship, and by the time my study leave began (around five months before exams), I had already completed classes for three subjects."

Chinmay's journey wasn't devoid of challenges—no champion's journey ever is! People who accept challenges and rise to the occasion become extraordinary. His grandma suffered a fracture during the intense preparation phase, and just ten days before the exam, his mom had a fall. Chinmay's biggest challenge, however, was being consistent in clocking the effective hours needed.

Being consistent for a week or even a month is easy, but six months is a marathon! In the initial three months, Chinmay clocked around six to eight hours per day; thereafter, he switched gears and began clocking 14–15 hours each day.

"Having both a long-term target and a daily target helps achieve consistency," says Chinmay.

No seed can flourish in the wrong ecosystem, and the ecosystem is as important for humans as it is for seeds.

"Studying on the terrace of my apartment was a huge contributing factor to my All India Rank! The trees and birds, the fresh air and good view— all of it helped enhance my effectiveness. I could comfortably study from 9 a.m. to 6 p.m. without getting tired."

"Where do most students go wrong? Give me only the most common mistake," I request.

Almost immediately, Chinmay replies, *"Ignoring ICAI modules is the single biggest mistake. Most faculty in private coaching centres teach based on weightage, and that is a risky proposition; you need to study everything—period! And anyway, only ICAI modules will help you for the Integrated Business Solution paper."*

According to him, an AIR mindset is all about wanting an extraordinary score. *"The aim shouldn't be to just pass. You need to aim really high. And to achieve that, you need to have confidence in what you're doing and confidence in yourself!"*

Every single rank holder I interviewed has their own way of dealing with distractions. Chinmay's philosophy is that a big goal saves you from swerving off the path. His mighty ambition led him to deactivate all his social media accounts, uninstall almost all apps, and focus solely on his preparations. When it comes to greatness, there's no free lunch—you need to earn every bit of it through extraordinary efforts.

I asked Chinmay for some insights that can help students in the exam hall, and he shares two important pointers:

1. Writing keywords in the question paper: This helps save a lot of time. You'll remember them when you first read the question, but later you might waste precious time trying to recall them.

2. Get a lot of writing practice: There's no substitute for this. Aim to write at least two to three 100-mark tests.

Sooner or later, life will knock us down, but we can always choose whether or not to stand back up.

And if you choose to stand back up, you'll become a hero—a champion and a leader like Chinmay! So, choose wisely!

SHE CAME, SHE SAW, SHE CONQUERED!

CA. Romitha

AIR 13 – Final – Dec 2021

Romitha cleared her IPCC when she was in her first year of college. With two years of college remaining—and two years for her final exams—she decided to pursue other courses. And guess what? She scored All India Ranks in her CS and CMA Intermediate! She then wanted to achieve a hat trick, so she scored a rank in CA Final!

Everything about Romitha is amusing! *"How did you choose CA in the first place?"* I ask, expecting a clichéd response, and she stunned me with a war cry: *"Since I scored great in 10th, my school compelled me to choose science, so I chose commerce. And since CA is the most challenging course in the commerce stream, I plunged into CA."* She came, she saw, she conquered!

Well, between seeing and conquering, there was a two-year stint of extreme focus and extraordinary effort! Romitha did her articleship in one of the Big 4 firms, and hence juggling office and studies was no easy feat!

"How did you even manage a Big 4 articleship and an AIR?" I ask with awe.

After a childlike laugh, she replies, *"You're not going to be busy all 365 days a year! You can compensate for the busy days by increasing your efforts on free days! And if you want greatness, you have to be willing to go the extra mile!"*

She makes everything sound so simple. Even her study strategies were simple!

Here are three study methods Romitha swears by:

1. Summary of adjustments: A two- to three-line summary of errors, new concepts, and tricky aspects.
2. Teaching method of learning: Studying as if you are teaching someone the concept deeply.
3. Working out past question papers: The questions in a textbook are sequenced chapter-wise, which makes them easier to crack, whereas in a 100-mark question paper the questions are jumbled and hence more challenging.

Nothing fancy, right? That's precisely what makes her a genius.

Leonardo da Vinci said, *"Simplicity is the ultimate sophistication."* *Steve Jobs* built his life around this quote, and Romitha is no different! She executed the ordinary with extraordinary focus and consistency.

So, did she aim for a rank?

"No! And my advice to my juniors is: rather than pressurising yourself by obsessing over a rank, focus on the process!" But even so, the preparation would have been stressful, right? *"The process itself was fun for me. It's important to enjoy the process. Have fun with learning."*

"Didn't you have any fear at all then?" I prod skeptically.

Her response is a poster-worthy quote: *"If you don't fear, you are fighting without purpose! Fear puts you on track; it motivates you to give your 100 percent."* Sounds like a war cry, doesn't it?

Giving our 100 percent means doing what needs to be done, even when we don't want to do it! Just because champions like Romitha learn to enjoy the process doesn't mean it was easy for them! Want audit evidence? Well, here's a quote penned by Romitha that I found on her Instagram page: *"Real pain for a warrior is not the visible wound, but the intangible efforts endured."* The single common denominator among all those featured in this book is incredible effort!

Romitha signs off with this beautiful piece of advice:

"The process is more beautiful than the results, so focus on the process. Even failure is beautiful, for it makes you stronger and shapes your future. The experience you gain from the process is far more valuable than the outcome."

I read this chapter to my dad and mom; and as soon as I finished, Dad wondered aloud, *"Who's she—a warrior or a zen master?"* Mom exclaimed, *"She's both!"*

THE JOURNEY

With no prior experience in writing or publishing, I set forth on this remarkable adventure seven months ago. While I strongly believed that this book would impact many CA students, little did I imagine that I would be its first beneficiary!

Each one of these extremely inspiring people sowed in me a spark of their greatness, and that spark has slowly but surely begun consuming me. I can now say with utmost confidence that if you light a lamp for someone else, it will also brighten your own path.

I treasure the memories of TNM Sir receiving me at the gate, MPV Sir moving to another chair so that it would be comfortable for me, GR Uncle removing my teacup, SD Bala Sir including my name in his celebrity list, the dozen texts from Amrut asking me if I need any help, and the calls and messages from almost every single one of them sharing their happiness on reading their stories—all memories I'll treasure for a lifetime!

I hope and pray that all of their wisdom guides you on your journey to greatness. As for me, I shall carry all the love and memories they've bestowed upon me as I continue to wander on the shores of love.

Lots of love,
P. Shandip Sabapathy
An eternal wanderer.

ABOUT THE AUTHOR

CA. P. Shandip Sabapathy is a Chartered Accountant by qualification, a farmer by vocation, and a speaker by passion. He has sat with the broken, healed the wounded, and inspired people toward greatness—and these, he considers, his true accomplishments.

He spent his formative years at Good Shepherd International School in Ooty. His academic credentials include a Bachelor of Commerce from PSG College of Arts & Science, a Master in Applied Psychology from Bharathiar University, and a specialisation in Positive Psychology from the University of Pennsylvania.

He has contested and won numerous speech contests conducted by Toastmasters International. His mentorship programme for CA students has produced innumerable success stories, including a few All India Ranks.

CA P. Shandip Sabapathy has addressed over a lakh people in the last decade and has trained executives of various organisations such as Ford India Ltd, HDFC Ltd, Milacron Moldmasters, Anamallais Toyota, Paragon, and others.

His ability to draw parallels from psychology and Eastern philosophy, to weave in humour, and to impart profound life lessons through interesting stories makes him a sought-after speaker in both academia and industry. His TEDx talk on "Finding and Sustaining Happiness" is a perfect testimony to his passion, purpose, and speaking prowess.

Contact details:
Phone no: +91 9489220202
Email ID: shandipwrites@gmail.com